PENGUIN BOOKS

REAL MAN TELLS ALL

Peter Nelson is a graduate of the Iowa Writers'
Workshop and is a recipient of a James Michener
Fellowship. His fiction and nonfiction have ap-
peared in, among other places, *Esquire, Harper's,
Seventeen, Redbook, Elle,* and *Ms.,* and for two
years he wrote the "His" column in *Mademoiselle.*
He lives in Northampton, Massachusetts.

PETER NELSON

■

Real Man Tells All

Confessions of an Eligible Bachelor

■

PENGUIN BOOKS

PENGUIN BOOKS
Published by the Penguin Group
Viking Penguin Inc., 40 West 23rd Street,
New York, New York 10010, U.S.A.
Penguin Books Ltd, 27 Wrights Lane,
London W8 5TZ, England
Penguin Books Australia Ltd, Ringwood,
Victoria, Australia
Penguin Books Canada Ltd, 2801 John Street,
Markham, Ontario, Canada L3R 1B4
Penguin Books (N.Z.) Ltd, 182–190 Wairau Road,
Auckland 10, New Zealand

Penguin Books Ltd, Registered Offices:
Harmondsworth, Middlesex, England

First published in Penguin Books 1988
Published simultaneously in Canada

Some of the selections of this book first appeared in
the *Chicago Tribune*, *Harper's Bazaar*, *Mademoiselle*, and *Ms*.

Grateful acknowledgment is made for permission to reprint
excerpts from the following copyrighted works:

"The Death of the Hired Man" from *The Poetry of Robert Frost*
edited by Edward Connery Lathem, published by Henry Holt and
Company, Inc. Copyright 1936 by Robert Frost.
Copyright © 1964 by Lesley Frost Ballantine.
Copyright © 1969 by Holt, Rinehart and Winston.

"Please Call Me Baby" by Tom Waits. © 1974
Fifth Floor Music, Inc.

Library of Congress Cataloging in Publication Data
Nelson, Peter, 1953–
Real man tells all.
1. Single men—Psychology.   2. Love.
3. Interpersonal relations.   I. Title.
HQ800.3.N45   1988   305.3'890652   87-29143
ISBN 0 14 01.1075 5

Printed in the United States of America by
R. R. Donnelley & Sons Company, Harrisonburg, Virginia
Set in Fairfield Medium
Designed by Victoria Hartman

To B.H., R.T., P.G., and Ellen

Contents

Introduction

■

Maybe it was the effect *A Connecticut Yankee in King Arthur's Court* had on me when I was a boy, my first exposure to any story about time travel, or maybe it's natural to seek the imaginary counsel of one's heroes—what else are they for?—but when the modern world becomes too much to take, or when I'm simply daydreaming and I go back in time, I often visit Mark Twain.

He's a little suspicious at first and not altogether overwhelmed by the idea that I've come from the future—where else could a time traveler come from? Eventually I win him over by bringing him thoughtful gifts from the present, Dove Bars and aerosol cans of Scotchguard to keep his suits white. He gives me cigars and signed first editions, and invites me to join him on a riverboat trip down the Mississippi, where we take turns at the wheel, sip bourbon, and chat about literature, politics, and world affairs. Nothing I tell him about politics or world affairs surprises him either, though it does partly amaze him, once I've explained nuclear weapons to him, and how many we have, that having the means to destroy mankind for over forty years, we have managed not to do so. Later in the evening, well into our cups, the conversation gets personal.

"Got a girl?" he asks.

"Sure," I say.

"Like her?"

"Like her?" I say, "I love her."

"Happy?"

"Sure," I say. "I mean, we're working on it. I mean, I suppose sometimes we have trouble ordering our priorities, balancing our individual needs with what we want out of our relationship, but the way we're making progress in finding ways to communicate, we're hopeful this thing is going to evolve into something that's satisfying and productive."

"I don't know about the future," he says, "but given that, my guess is, if I could put a saddle on the source of what you just said, I'd win the Kentucky Derby. What you mean is, you're not happy."

"We're happy," I insist. "I mean, most of the time it's great. And when it isn't great, we work on it."

"You work on it," he says.

"Sure," I say. "We set aside some time to discuss how we feel and what we want, and what we're not getting, and what's working and what isn't."

"Ohhhhh," he says. "You fight."

"No," I say. "Not exactly. We just think, in the 1980s, that it's important to . . . well, to understand what you're going through while you're going through it, take it apart, analyze it, examine it, put it back together, correct our mistakes, improve ourselves, maybe. *Learn* about ourselves, through our relationships, so that we can grow."

"I see," he says. "You enjoy this?"

"No," I say. "Not necessarily. We don't always want to, but sometimes we have to. Don't *you* ever feel the need to work on your relationship?"

"Naw," he says. "We just fight."

"Must be nice," I say.

"I live in a simpler time," he says. He puts his thumb to his nose and wiggles his fingers at me.

"Go ahead," I say, "rub it in."

Of course, in this fantasy conversation I do not tell him that at one point in my life, I supplied people with information, opinions, and anecdotes to help them work on their relationships—that I wrote a men's column for a women's magazine. The idea for this book began with those columns. I always knew I'd write about love and romance, since by and large it's what I think about almost all the time, but I can't say I ever expected to write a monthly column, or quite what to make of it. Even in the present, I've never known quite how to put it when people ask me what I did.

"I wrote one of those men's confession columns," I say.

You get an assortment of reactions. One woman friend said, "Really? I always thought those were written by women using male pen names. I thought it was sounding more masculine."

"Thanks," I said.

"But only a little."

The most common reaction is *"You?"* Not just from people who know me, either. Total strangers raise an eyebrow and say, *"You?"* Why do they doubt me? What do they expect? Some Professor Higgins-ish character in a paisley smoking jacket, with the ascot and the monocle, dictating over his shoulder to his personal secretary while sucking thoughtfully on a pipe, gazing out the bay window at grazing fauns? I often write poetry that way, but never nonfiction. Or maybe they expect a Miss Lonelyhearts type, meek and mild, button-down shirts and sweater-vests and Hush Puppies. I'm not saying I'm Joe Super-Macho (*that* would be a pen name), but last summer I was wearing jeans, a T-shirt, and cowboy boots, hadn't shaved for a few days, and a trucker in a gas station asked me, "You driving that rig parked yonder?" "Nope," I said with as good a drawl as I could muster, and walked—no, I moseyed—with pride around the corner of the gas station, where I got back in my girlfriend's pale yellow VW Rabbit and drove away. Being took for a trucker is perhaps the highest compliment a man can pay another man. Ten four, good buddy, lay the hammer down, catch you on the flip-flop. Whatever impression I give, it isn't what people expect of a men's columnist. *You?*

I understand their doubts, actually, because the first thing I thought when *Mademoiselle* offered me the job was, "Me?" *"Me?"* Was it laughable? Were my ex-girlfriends not all lining up outside hardware stores at the crack of dawn to buy shovels to take to cemeteries to dig graves to climb down into and spin before they were even dead? Of course they were. Me? An expert in relationships?

When I was a kid, I liked art and baseball. I figured I'd grow up to be the Minnesota Twins' left fielder or else work in advertising. I asked my mother what was a job you could do art in, and she said advertising. No one, I do not think, ever spends his free time in kindergarten dreaming to one day write a men's column for a women's magazine, penning cogent little character sketches of his classmates, like, "Katy was an attractive girl, witty, bright smile, completely toilet-trained, and yet, when I spread my rug on the floor next to her at nap time, she seemed suddenly leery of the imposed intimacy, as if her apparent easy confidence were a false facade."

Maybe I was curious, though, about why girls seemed so different from boys. Why they had longer hair. Why they weren't supposed to roughhouse, while it was okay for us to. Why we took baths at separate times. Why we had a crossbar on our bicycles that caused excruciating pain when we rode our bikes off a curb, slipped off the seat and fell on the crossbar, while girls' bikes didn't. I liked napping next to them, but I couldn't explain it. I used to sneak up behind girls I didn't even know in kindergarten and kiss them on the shoulder blades. (To be perfectly honest, I still get the urge to do nothing more than that, especially to women in strapless gowns at fancy parties, but now I restrain myself.) I kissed Diane Lindermann on the lips in first grade when she taught me how to tie my shoes. I liked girls, and I wanted them to like me, when I grew up to be a baseball-playing ad man. But an advice columnist? Me?

I questioned my qualifications. I didn't want to come on like someone who says, "Marriage? Why sure, I've been married seven times—ask me anything—I'm an *expert* on marriage." Being married seven times, to me, means you're no good at it. At the same time, a guy who's been happily married to his high school sweetheart for twenty years would only be qualified to describe one situation, and if he's really been that happy for that long, I'd doubt he's ever had much cause to think long and hard about it. He's no expert either—he's just lucky. I was supposed to write about my feelings? What about all the girlfriends who'd told me I was opaque about my feelings, wanted me to share my true and deep ones, when in fact I thought I'd just told them what my true and deep ones were, as clearly as I thought I could make them? If the women who knew me weren't completely satisfied with my ability to communicate, how could I hope to satisfy a wide readership of women who didn't? I asked myself what Mark Twain would have done. Didn't Hemingway write for *Cosmo*?

Events conspired to persuade me to do it. With the money from the first three articles I sold to *Mademoiselle*, I joined an HMO and finally had an operation to correct the damage from a knee injury which, two years earlier, had dimmed forever my hopes of playing left field for the Minnesota Twins. Before the operation, I met with the orthopedic surgeon, who, it turned out, had a bad back. Then the woman who took my X rays was wearing a wig, presumably because her hair had all fallen out. Then I met the physical therapist, who seemed anorexic. The ophthalmologists all wore glasses. I already knew some of the psychiatrists who worked at my HMO, and half of them were nuts. Right around then, a warehouse full of fire extinguishers burned down. Fine, I thought. I'm an expert. What the hell.

Maybe I was holding unreasonably high expectations for myself, the same high expectations perhaps that some women have when they think words coming from a man's mouth (or from his word processor) are going to suddenly and finally explain everything and resolve all misunderstandings. We're not *supposed* to communicate that well, or understand completely with perfect clarity. We're not even that clear in our own minds, seeking self-understanding. Maybe some day in the year 4000, when we all wear flowing white robes and have bald heads the size of basketballs and communicate telepathically or with blinking lights on our wristbands, maybe then life will be calm and fair and just, but for now all we can do is grope around doing the best we can and trying to be honest. Growing older, you begin to suspect, with resignation and relief, that everything is just what it looks like and is going to stay that way, that tension and conflict and misunderstanding are there for a reason, all part of the same dynamism that attracts us to each other in the first place. You can't really win, but you can lose if you stop trying, so the idea is to stay curious, hope for the occasional breakthrough, take naps when you're tired, and eat square meals. Slightly lowered expectations from when I was young.

And anyway, questions about love are, have always been, and always will be vague and fuzzy, too hard to frame, never mind answer. They're almost better couched in songs than in prose. Why love at all? Why this person and not that one? In high school, I had the horrible fear, now that I was heading into puberty, that, against my wishes, I was going to fall in love with someone I didn't want to be in love with, that I'd fall for some green-toothed brutal biker mama (no offense to any green-toothed brutal biker mamas out there) and have to stay forever with someone I didn't like. Love was such a mysterious force that I feared it could do that to me. I mean, what the hell is it? Where does it come from? Where does it go? Why can't you know? People want Ten Surefire Signs That He's in Love, when I doubt there's even one that can't be faked, and the belief in surefiredness is self-delusion, a wish that things weren't so complicated. It is, after all, the wish of the 1980s. You don't want to undercomplicate the issues by putting them in nutshells, misserving the truth. Still, people turn to magazine columns for advice, even if the best advice is a kind of lie, a slick promise that love can be explained and problems remedied by the simple application of common sense. Everybody knows love defies common sense.

People write to you for advice when you do one of these columns. I was once desperately in love and wrote to Ellen Goodman, a syndicated columnist for the *Boston Globe*, asking her for love advice, and she writes about politics, not love. I only asked her because she's so smart. She said she didn't know any answers, but that I should keep asking the questions. There's no telling where people in love trouble will turn. In a very funny, wise, underrated, and unfairly forgotten movie called *Modern Romance*, Albert Brooks ends up uncontrollably pouring his heart out to highway tollbooth operators and shoe salesmen.

Most of the letters I got thanked me for finally saying things my readers had never heard the men they know say before. When I read women who write about being women, I know I'm looking for secrets and feel as though I'm eavesdropping, the fly-on-the-wall at an eighth-grade girls' slumber party, hearing what they really think. The goal of a man writing about being a man would be to provide the same perspective, a confession without trying to be overtly defensive or apologetic, though you're going to be a little of each most of the time. It's daunting to, in effect, speak for men on behalf of all the enigmatic husbands or boyfriends who can't or don't want to own up to anything. The emotional reticence of the American male is well documented—you'd be hard-pressed to open your car door and not hit a woman willing to testify to the fact of it—but I don't know what explains it. Sometimes I think the women I know use conversation, with each other at least, as a way of discovering what they think or feel about a subject, a freely participatory verbal exploration, actual discourse. They talk to establish sympathy, support the group and each other, enhance the bonding. Men aren't into that. We see that kind of conversation as an exercise in commiseration that might make people feel good but doesn't go anywhere, so who needs it? Some of the conversations I've had with other men come off like a William F. Buckley "Firing Line" show, where no one says anything they haven't already thought out and preworded, or in Buckley's own case, published five or six books about. Men use conversation as an opportunity to state a position, joust and spar and establish a defendable tenet, and support the group, therein, by constructing a fortress of truisms to believe in, while staying interpersonally competitive and individually protected. Linguists studying the way men talk to women in groups say men tend to change the subject at will on women, or interrupt them, while women speak tentatively or deferentially, qualifying themselves and underscoring words while saying supportive things. Little wonder we have trouble, one on one.

In my own case, in those late-night conversations when women I've loved have said they don't know what I'm *feeling*, all I ever have to say is what I have to *guess* I'd say, *if* I knew what I was talking about. I feel uncomfortable when I don't have a clear position. I'm never totally sure of myself. How, for instance, can I explain that sometimes I feel the strong need to get away from someone I love? How can someone feel repelled and drawn at the same time? I don't get it, but I want to get it before I talk about it. This, I've learned, through a whole series of those late-night conversations, doesn't wash—you have to jump in with both feet and take a wild stab at it, right out loud, if only because while you're mulling it over silently, other people are getting lonely waiting. In that sense, this book is a compilation of distilled wild stabs. Unmix that metaphor if you can.

Much of it reads like a long personal ad—my perfect woman, my perfect date, whatever—and many of the letters I'd received were responses in kind. I think I could travel around the country for a year and not run out of places to stay, from women who wrote and said, "If you're ever in El Reno, Oklahoma, give me a call" (sorry, I've been there), or "If you're ever in Yellowknife. . . ." Ninety-nine percent of the people who wrote were women; 75 percent were single; maybe half were divorced, in their early thirties. I could tell which ones were divorced because they would send photographs which were the normal three inches tall but only an inch and a half wide, and the woman in the photograph would have a man's hand on her hip, opposite the side of the picture where the man owning the hand used to be before she cut the snapshot in half with scissors. It isn't hard to imagine how palpably satisfying cutting the picture in half must have been. If only you could crop an ex- from your life as easy as that. Husband? What husband? Never heard of the guy. Photographs of women kissing their dogs, when I wrote a column saying I liked women who liked dogs. A professional head shot from a ballerina in New Jersey. A hair ad from a model in Bermuda. No lingerie shots, just nice, sweet people.

I'd get phone calls too, long distance even, before I stopped listing where I lived in my bio. My favorite was one Friday night, about nine-thirty, from a girl named Kim, whose parents had grounded her but who, I guessed, had forgotten to take her phone away, so she was getting revenge by running up the bill. She wanted to know if I was single, and how old I was. That month, the magazine had used a photograph of a forlorn-looking guy to illustrate an article I'd written, and Kim wanted to know if that was a picture of me.

"No," I said, "that was some male model in New York."

"Oh," she said, her voice loaded with disappointment.

"Sorry."

"Well, uhh . . . what do you look like?" she asked.

"Well," I said, "I have curly hair and a mustache."

"Uh-huh," she said. She was still disappointed.

"Maybe I look a little like that guy in the Camel Light cigarette ads," I said. The guy in the khaki clothes who they always show with a rope over his shoulder and a butt hanging from the corner of his mouth, and he's usually pulling a Jeep up a dry river bed (what's wrong with this picture?), which may be a good ad for cigarettes but not good for Jeeps, I don't suppose.

"Really?" she said, brightly. "That's okay."

"Thanks," I said.

Later, I wrote an article entitled "An Unmarried Man," to go along with a feature the magazine was doing on the Fifty Most Eligible Bachelors. I was asked to come to New York and have my picture taken—I thought to go with the article, not to be one of the eligibles. They ended up running it, right alongside Don Johnson and Pat Metheny and Jellybean Benitez. I'm surprised anybody called me at all after that, because I looked dweebier than I usually do in photographs—I'd walked twenty-five blocks down Broadway to get to the photography studio, and was in my normal New York state of mind, wanting to chuck anyone who got in my way into the paths of oncoming cabs or bite the feet off pigeons. New York does this to me. At any rate, the photo ran, and friends gave me no end of grief about it. I told them it had all been a big mistake, that I misunderstood and thought I was being nominated as one of the fifty most *illegible* bachelors. That very week, the phone rang, and a sultry woman's voice came over the line. The voice tried to be seductive.

"I'd like to speak to Peter Nelson, the most handsome eligible bachelor in this month's *Mademoiselle*," she said.

"Give me a break, Mom," I said. "Did you really think I wasn't going to recognize your voice?" Baby seals in a rookery of *ten thousand* seals can still pick out their mother's honk in the din.

I did not intend to write glorified personal ads, though it's the nature of any writing to make yourself look a little better than you know or suspect you are. I was sitting in a bar booth with a bunch of guys once, when an old buddy named Jim asked, "So what kinds of things do you actually do in this column you write?" "Well, Jim," I said, "actually, I spend most of my time apologizing for guys like you." It got a big laugh, and in truth, there's nothing wrong with Jim that isn't wrong with any other guy you could name (well, there is, but I'm not saying what), but in truth, writing about men for women does end up being a chance to be the spokesman for everyone's favorite whipping boy in the eighties. Women's magazines are not against men, not when they run articles like "How to Bag Your Limit of Stud" or "*Cosmo* Reveals the Secret to Your Happiness—Pierce Brosnan's Home Phone Number." Even *Ms.* isn't antimen. There are pieces I'd like to write—not in this book—which celebrate manhood, our silly and/or noble habits, "Why I Love to Belch and Play Poker" or "Zen Softball—How to Increase Your Runs Buddha-ed In"; but for editorial purposes I have limited myself to areas of "gender interface" (as Alexander Haig would probably put it), addressing the problems, or dwelling apologetically on the negative things about us. For a column on infidelity, for example, I read a statistic that suggested perhaps as many as 90 percent of all married men may cheat on their wives. Okay, this is a fact that's hard to defend.

At the same time, a woman friend, Beth, years ago told me a story of another woman who, in mid-life, looked at a photograph of herself and her kids and hubby and ranch-style home in the 'burbs one day and realized she was living a lie of a life, that this was never what *she* wanted, not what she thought dropping out of college to marry the man she loved at the time would lead to. She felt she was a victim of other people's expectations, of society's, of outdated traditions, so she left her family and went back to college to finish her degree. Beth held this middle-aged coed up to me as a feminist hero, and I could see how she'd think that way, and I'd even partly agree, but I had to point out to Beth that the woman who went back to college had done almost exactly what lots of historically villainized husbands have done, ditched the family when they became convinced they were living a lie and it wasn't for them. I asked why a woman who abandons her home can be lionized when a man reacting to the same impulses almost never is? Different circumstances, but that different?

So married men cheat, but often with women who know they're married. And married women cheat, but only half the percentage as men. We're screwed up, but who isn't? We are violent, men and women both. I read of a study which said more children are abused by women than by men. We act on fantasies we shouldn't, we have hang-ups, insecurities, fears, prejudices, but we are noble too, have lofty sentiments, are occasionally kind to each other. We deserve to have our failings looked at with compassion and forgiveness. We have blind spots of our own, even more when we try to see through someone else's eyes. If, in the year 4000, we ever reach a point in our flowing robes and bald heads where men and women really do understand each other, and there's no divorce, no sadness, no fighting, and we all stop making mistakes, *then* I'm moving. I can't think of anything less interesting than a perfect world. Not that I'm worried. I would go back in time and tell Mark Twain I was wrong.

"You enjoy this?" he asks. "Working on relationships?"

Yes. No doubt there are relationships today which fail, but which would succeed if one could transport them lock, stock, and barrel back to simpler times. But you can't, and I like it here anyway. No romantic failure, however heartbreaking, is a waste of time. Love is infinitely fascinating—why we're good, why we're wicked, why we care in the first place, why we fail to show it, how we succeed when we do, where our ideas come from, how we fool ourselves, why we can't admit it, where we're different, and what it all adds up to when we get together.

Who am I to write about this stuff? Hopefully a reasonably normal person, born male on the eighth of February 1953, in Minneapolis, Minnesota, who stared out the window of the green Studebaker taking him home from the hospital and was heard to say, "I wonder what the story is with this love thing." It came out as a gurgle, but that's what I meant. I write about love for the same reason people read about it—I want to see how it's going to turn out. No matter how heartbroken I've ever been, and I've been steamrolled by experts, I've always thought, sure it hurts, but it's just so damn *interesting*. I "work on relationships" on paper, I suppose, trying to combine stories I've heard, things I've read, and lessons I've learned the hard way, to take some of the drudgery out of working on relationships, which, when you get right down to it, is nice work if you can get it.

Why We're Like This

■

An Unmarried Man

■

We're young and free. We stride the earth like colossi, leaving a trail of broken hearts behind us. We go where we want, when we please, down the fast lane in little red convertibles that shine in the sun, on roads leading to adventure, past the point of no return—that's where we feel at home. We're your best dream and your worst nightmare. One day we might be your whole world. The next day we're gone. We couldn't stay.

We're bachelors.

7 A.M.: I wake up. The other side of the bed looks as vast and empty as Nebraska. There's a two-foot-high pile of dirty clothes on the dresser, cascading to the floor. I make a mental note, illegible because I'm barely awake, to tell my butler to clean it up, and then I suddenly remember—I don't have a butler. I must be confusing myself with Prince Charles again. Now, *there* was a bachelor's bachelor. He could walk right up to a woman and say, "Buy you a drink? I'm heir to one of the largest family fortunes in the world." Even Charlie's married now, two kids, tied down, wife goes dancing without him. Sucker.

What do I have to do today? (1) Pick up clothes. Sharon, a woman I just met at a party, is coming over. I don't want her to think I'm the clichéd bachelor-slob. Though I am. If we get as far as the bedroom. Or the kitchen. Or the bathroom. (2) Clean whole house. My dog, Stella, the only female in residence, greets me as if I'm

3

Ulysses home from the Trojan Wars, just as she does every morning. She knocks me down with love, for free. No strings attached. Unlike some women I can think of, she doesn't order me around, either, try to shape me up, or call me to account. Which might actually be useful, sometimes.

7:15 A.M.: Morning toilet. I get on the scale, look in the mirror. Question: Will being tanner make me look thinner? Shaving my mustache will make me look younger. Also dopier. Not today. I shave extra carefully. I need to avoid conspicuous gashes on my face tonight. Nice, though, to see my old friend Mr. Pimple is back; since junior high school, he has always managed to show up on the mornings of big dates. Sharon will, of course, see it and hate my guts immediately. I shower, crooning the Beatles' "I'm a Loser." (3) Buy Comet to use on tub. Bubble bath, too? Girls love that stuff. Maybe I should wait until the second date, though? Boy Scouts' training: be prepared.

7:30 A.M.: I look out the window at my embarrassingly old, beat-up station wagon. Sharon will be driving herself over tonight in her brand-new Spider 2000. (4) Hide car around corner. I was supposed to be making dinner, but there is nothing much in the refrigerator. When I was in college, I'd have a case of beer and a bottle of catsup in it. Now I have beer, catsup, a pack of Fenway Franks from a year ago, but they keep forever if you don't open them, right? I've got "lite" margarine that doesn't melt when you put it on toast, a foil-wrapped morsel of cream cheese that has turned to terra-cotta, and thirty or forty nearly empty bottles and jars and cans of sauces left over from other meals cooked for other dates: hoisin sauce, oyster sauce, fancy mustards, chutneys, barbecue and steak sauces, and a bottle of French dressing that looks as if it goes all the way back to the storming of the Bastille. I toss it. Women hate being served rotten food. No stomach for mold whatsoever. (5) Buy groceries.

The menu question is, Do you make something feminine for her, like steamed dove breasts in lemon butter on a bed of parsley with a Perrier spritzer, or do you give her meat loaf on a board with a bucket of grog, to see what kind of stuff she's made of? This time, I'll go with my strength—chili. Chili just spicy enough to make her upper lip moist. If she can take it, I'll know she won't blanch when she learns about the rest of me—when I "open up." Women go nuts over guys who open up.

8 A.M.: Breakfast. To this wild and crazy guy, that means one thing. The International House of Pancakes. Exotic dishes from foreign lands, "unique burgers" on the menu, like "bacon cheese-burger." How unique. It's my office. I know all the waitresses: Diane, with the luxurious long hair bound in a health-department bun; Julie, so quiet you can hardly hear her; and Annie, my favorite because she's always laughing at some private joke she refuses to reveal to me, no matter how much I try to flirt it out of her. Maybe she's kinky? I value my daily contact with these women more than they know. I see them more often than any of my other women friends. I could really, uh . . . date . . . Annie.

Sharon Sharon Sharon. Bright, funny, attractive, athletic, loves to sail, something I know nothing about because I don't sail because I can't swim because I can't even float. This date will be a disaster. (6) Call Matt and get some sailing jargon. Why catastrophize? Because of previous catastrophes, like the time my friend Jack and I had a blind double-date with his friend Rick's sister Debra and her friend Susan, except Rick didn't know or tell Jack that Debra and Susan were black-leather, studded-collar vampire lesbians— really perfectly nice people, but maybe not precisely the dates Jack and I had in mind. To think of the time we spent, cleaning his place for that one.

10 A.M. to 5 P.M.: I clean. The floors are embarrassing, but there's no time to sand and revarnish them. I sweep, mop, wash the melted soap from the soap dish, make all the toothbrushes point bristles-left, do the laundry, and at long last, for Sharon (some day, I hope she will appreciate my sacrifice), I throw away all my worn-out boxer shorts. I change the sheets, make the bed, and wash the dishes, putting the ones that won't come clean in a drawer she's not likely to open. I shop, then start the chili. I once made a woman chili, and I was so nervous I forgot to add the beans, resulting in something like Mexican spaghetti sauce. (7) Remember the beans.

I can definitely feel that predate adrenaline kicking in. Onions, mushrooms, peppers, celery (a secret ingredient), sirloin cut in squares (no ground beef for this girl), and bacon, with grease. Geez. There's certainly a lot of chili here. Maybe there'll be some left over for Ellen or maybe Amy. Or . . .

Sharon Sharon Sharon. Sometimes, it's hard to focus on one person at one time. As my friend Andy said, "I have to admit it— I want to sleep with every woman in the world." He's working his way through the Manhattan telephone book. He's made it to the P's already, and he's my age. Sometimes he lies awake at night wondering how many women there are who don't have phones. And then he turns around and tells me, "I just can't find one I want to settle down with—maybe I'm too picky?" It's frightening to think what his track record would be like if he weren't so "selective." What's even more frightening is that I understand exactly what he's saying. Sharon.

7 p.m.: One more shower for luck while the chili simmers. Then it's costume time. Something simple is best, for starters. I try pastels, but it's all wrong—I look as if I just stepped off the professional golf tour. Black is too rock star/starving painter. Definitely not a suit. I opt for a pale blue shirt with small grey checks and a white sweater, clean blue jeans. Eugene O'Neill at the Cape. God, it all sucks, but there's no time. Just when I notice how stupid my hair looks, the doorbell rings.

Sharon looks a hundred times better than I do.

"Oh no," I say. Self-deprecating candor is my only way out. "You look about a hundred times better than me. Wait here while I go change." She's wearing one of those huge white shirts, wide red belt, narrow pants, her hair artfully mussed. Great. I go conservative; she goes foxy. Sharon is so perfect it's scary. Thank God she brought the wrong wine—Liebfraumilch doesn't exactly go with chili. We're on an equal footing again.

Over dinner, I fall back on my training. My mother always said to look people in the eye and ask them questions about themselves. Sharon tells me about her family. I tell her about my family, and everything's going okay and all, but I can't help thinking about how many times I've trotted these stories out before. I've probably even told them in exactly the same way, same inflections, hand gestures. It's as if I've been reciting to women the first few pages of a long book—one that's all about me. I think about how no one has ever managed to finish the book, and I sure as hell don't know why. After all, it's a good book. Isn't it? Even women I've known a long time, and the one I lived with, have put it down. I'm tired of opening chapters and first paragraphs.

Uh-oh. Sharon is looking at me as if I'm weird. Women hate it when you suddenly get quiet and morose and drift off. Good sign she noticed, though.

8:45 P.M.: It's going fine, but we decide to go to a movie anyway— her idea. Maybe she's afraid we're going to run out of things to say. I readily concur, because I don't like awkward silences either. So we head for the theater, and the lights go down just as we take our seats. Man, is this familiar. I've been taking dates to movies for almost twenty years. I *know* this. Where to put the popcorn, how not to set the soda on the arm where I might knock it over, even how to recover if I do—I spilled Coke on someone once, and there was nothing to wipe it up with, so I quickly splashed some on myself, just to make things even. It left quite an impression, the woman told me later. Just when I'm feeling right at home, the guy sitting in front of us asks the woman he's with if she goes to the movies often, and he's at least fifty years old. Imagine that, taking dates to movies when you're fifty. Twenty more years of this? There's a fate that wants escaping.

11:30 P.M.: Drinks afterward. She has V.O. on the rocks, a very good sign. She wants to know what things taste like, pure and undiluted. Sweet drinks with obnoxious names—the ones where they throw a quart of ice cream, half a wedding cake, and an ounce of brandy into a blender and then serve it in a glass the size of a birdbath—shake my faith in the people who order them.

We are clearly warming to each other. She tells me more about her family. Her sister is getting married in a few months. Sharon had a bet with her sister over who'd marry first. I mention that my baby sister is getting married soon too, which will make me the only kid left unwed. Everyone will be staring at me at the reception, wondering what's wrong with me. The only way to avoid that, I say, would be to bring a date, and would Sharon like to come? Talk about putting a woman in an awkward position. I laugh, to let her know I'm half kidding, because it's our first date, and who really cares what people think, but . . .

Holy mother of cows. It's our first date, and here we are, talking about marriage! With her just one side of thirty and me the other—marriage. The "M" word. A shiver goes down my spine. A Stygian blackness spreads like ink inside me. Really. A Stygian blackness.

1 A.M.: We go home. Maybe she hasn't noticed me withdraw-ing—hanging back in cowardice—ever since the chimera of the "M" word raised its ugly head. She's extremely bright—surely she's noticed. Maybe she feels the same way. She's still smiling at me though, and seems to like me some, maybe a lot. She could just be the one. It's much too soon, even if it is all in my head. And of course, I'm expected to ask her to spend the night, which I might do if she weren't such a palpable threat to my singularity. Involvement is best nipped in the bud. The bigger it is, the harder to nip. I don't want something serious until I'm ready to be serious.

Then we reach the kiss part. What is as holy and wonderful as kissing someone for the first time? You can tell a lot from a kiss. Sharon, I know right away, has done this before. We take turns acting and reacting, leading and following. Sharon kisses kind of like Roxanne did in eighth grade, with a touch of Carol from my junior year in college, and yet, most of it is entirely new. What is kissing? Putting our softest parts in proximity to our most danger-ous, lips to teeth. Richard III baring his chest and handing Lady Anne the sword.

"Thank you for the chili," she says.

"Thank *you* for the chili," I say. There is a spot in the lower left corner of her mouth that I missed, so I have to kiss her all over again. I feel silly and happy, and only partly self-conscious, and I change my mind. "So . . ." (I know this pause like the back of my hand) ". . . you want to come up and . . . kiss some more?"

"Yes," she says. "But let's not."

"And say we did." I'm disappointed and relieved at the same time. She has definitely done this sort of thing before. Her caution is encouraging. "I want to see you again," I tell her. She says she wants to see me too, that I should call her.

1:45 A.M.: It's hard to get to sleep. The voices in my head, already weighing the possibilities with Sharon against the fear of commitment, are loud and unabating. The future is unknowable, so I concentrate on what I know. I know I'm lonely. I feel that someone should be here. Something lasting and strong should happen to me. I feel weary of the single life. I'm sick of repeating myself. I'm tired of feeling everything I do is a practiced trick to impress someone—I want someone to say, "Stop it, relax, I'll love you forever anyway." Where did I get the idea a bolt of lightning would hit me, telling me what to do? Think of anything else, think of work. Then, before I close my eyes, I look next to me, and there it is again.

Nebraska.

Big fields of dry brown prairie grass, as far as the eye can see.

(8) Call Sharon in the morning.

We are men without women, bachelors young and free. We travel the fast lane, but we still can't get away. We're lone wolves, and we howl at the moon, and we're going to keep howling until somebody hears us. We live the lives we've chosen. Or the lives that have chosen us. We're bachelors.

The Difference Between
Men and Dogs

∎

"Men are dogs," Elizabeth said. "All men are dogs."

"That's hardly fair," I said. "I mean, I appreciate the compliment, but I don't know what you have against dogs."

She huffed off. Home to her cat, no doubt. Women like cats because cats act as if they understand women. And they act as role models for women, displaying a dignified aloofness, full of love and affection, but pride also, a sureness of self, a gracefulness in a world of dogs that women can appreciate.

I am a dog man. I haven't gone a year in the last twenty-seven years without living in the company of at least one dog. I didn't appreciate Elizabeth's comments. I mean, I think I can tell the difference between men and dogs by now.

Dogs shed on your rugs, furniture, and clothes. White dogs shed only on black sweaters, and dark dogs on light sweaters. You can't keep dogs from shedding, but you can dye them the same color as your sweaters. Men will leave hairs here and there, but not as much. In the sink, or sticking to the sides of bathtubs. Dogs also have fleas, while men don't and are generally much cleaner, having only the occasional cigar. Dogs would rather have fleas than smoke cigars. Men can be trained not to smoke cigars, but it takes patience and firmness. Hit him on the nose with a rolled-up newspaper, point to an ashtray, and say, "Put it out!" and he probably will. Not always the first time, but with repetition.

Dogs embarrass you in public, knock over plants, trip old ladies, sniff at the crotches of total strangers, hump people's legs, or lick themselves. Men sometimes try to inconspicuously realign their boxer shorts in public. We also wear plaid pants on golf courses, walk around with little pieces of toilet paper stuck to our faces, and drink so much that we tell bad jokes in loud voices.

Dogs are not as bright as men. They managed to beat man into orbit in the late fifties, but have since fallen far behind in the space race, and are not expected to land a dog on the moon in the foreseeable future. You can fool them easily by spelling things, like "Whose turn is it to take S-P-O-T for a W-A-L-K?" If a woman at a dinner party says, in front of her husband, "Oh, by the way, Louise, I didn't tell you, did I? I'm having an A-F-F-A-I-R with B-O-B," her husband may well catch on. Then again, if he doesn't, she's probably doing the right thing.

Dogs bite when threatened. In some urban areas, human bites now outnumber dog bites, though the statistics never say what percentage of which sex is doing the biting. Dogs will bark, to avoid conflict, while men resort to biting sarcasm, to invoke it, and in general are much more vicious than dogs. Dogs only bite the moment it occurs to them to do so, and then forget about it. Men have been known to lay elaborate long-range revenge plots that continue long after the offense has passed. Men also wage war and build nuclear bombs. Dogs lack the funding to build bombs, but knowing them as well as I do, my guess is, give a dog all the money in the world, and he'll invent new rubber chew toys, not new weapons.

There are similarities. Dogs are elated when you feed them, and so are men. Dogs can't prepare their own food, and come to you with big puppy-dog eyes. Men could prepare their own food, but would still rather come to you with big puppy-dog eyes. Dogs show their gratitude better than men, though. They push their faces right into the bowl, tails wagging, until they're covered with food and the room is a mess. Men are messy, but not as endearingly so.

Dogs will keep you warm in bed. Sometimes my dog, Stella, will lick the salt from my hand as I fall asleep, until I start to drift off, dream a little, feel some weird warm wet sensation on my hand,

and wake up all of a sudden, thinking, "Oh my God—what the hell is that?" Men will keep women warm in bed, though there are probably times when women wake up suddenly, look at the hairy face on the pillow next to them in shock, and say, "Oh my God—what the hell is that?"

The dog's second greatest virtue is that he will take on anything to protect you, race headlong into a pitch-black basement to fend off burglars, alien invaders—he doesn't care. A dog in Duluth, chained to a tree, broke its chain to protect its master from an attacking black bear. Men share this virtue and will do pretty much whatever we can to protect the ones we love.

The dog's chief virtue is his faithfulness. If you should die, and no one comes to your house for weeks, a dog would rather starve to death than eat your body. Unlike, say, cats. Cat lovers argue that this speaks in favor of cats, and perhaps it does, but if it does, then I'd still rather own a dog.

Even though some dogs will, like some men, run away, as a rule men are less faithful than dogs. Dogs are emotionally short-sighted, and don't think to look beyond the love at hand, the one that feeds them and scratches them on the head. A dog capable of jumping five feet in the air can be kept inside a three-foot fence, as long as he doesn't know he could vault a five-foot one if he wanted to.

There are also dogs fully aware of how high they can jump who choose not to.

"Not all men are dogs," I told Elizabeth. "But a few good ones are."

The Naked Truth:
Why Men Like *Playboy*

■

I'm eleven and it's summer. My pals and I get on our bikes, go down to Victor Peabody's drugstore, and wait for Victor to go into the back to make a prescription. Paul works for Victor as a soda jerk, and keeps lookout behind the counter. He'll cough to warn us if Victor comes back up front. We sneak over to the magazine rack and pore over the *Playboy*s. Incredible. Simply unbelievable stuff.

"I seen a girl like that once," McCool says. "Through a window."

"Liar," Jay says. It's hard to know when McCool is lying, though— he's the J.D. of the group, but some of his lies could be true. One year he bought us cherry Cokes and malts all summer, until we learned he was stealing the money from the old lady who'd hired him to cut her grass. Paul coughs, and we put the magazine back quick and leave. That night in bed, I'm an Arctic explorer at the North Pole, and an airplane full of *Playboy* bunnies crash-lands, and the only way they can possibly stay alive is to take their clothes off and get in my special sleeping bag with me. . . .

No one wonders what boys get out of *Playboy*, and no one wonders why low-class, macho-slob types read "those magazines." But nice guys? At the newsstand in Harvard Square, Cambridge, Massachusetts—a place crawling with smart people—the two top-selling monthly magazines are *Penthouse* and *Playboy*. Women might well wonder why mature, well-educated, sophisticated guys love to look at pictures of naked women. Don't they know better?

Sure. Most do, but when has knowing better stopped anybody? The civilized part of our brain builds cities and writes symphonies, and "knows better," but the libidinous side of our nature resents being denied pleasure and begs to be recognized. We are not celibate monks—in a way, celibacy is as perverted as, well, perversion. We are all of high and low character. Maybe you couldn't be one without the other. Anyway, the conflict is inexorably there. Opening a girlie magazine can feel like a temporary truce. For me, anyway, part of the fun is knowing I'm still violating a taboo, nervously anticipating Paul's warning cough, in a way that seems harmless, just me alone, looking at a picture, not hurting anybody.

In private, face to face, one on one with a centerfold, nobody here but the two of us, I first respond to the beauty; these women are no less incredible to me now than they were when I was eleven. The freshness, the richer-than-life skin tones, the bright smiles, the artificial photographic voodoo that they do so well, combine to stun. The context is different, but the form is the same as in Greek statues or Rubens paintings. People who say the models are plasticized, boring, mono-dimensional, fabricated, and virtually the same from month to month aren't really talking about what the women in pictures look like so much as where they might fit in comparison or proportion to the real world and real women, or the social roles real women play. The women in the pictures, taken from context, are pretty women, something even antipornography advocates might admit. You can look at the pictures and say, "What's so wrong about admiring beauty—how is this so terribly different from Botticelli's *Venus* or Michelangelo's *David*? You can question the character of a man who values a woman's beauty above her other qualities, but I'm not sure how to assail the definition of physical beauty itself—a youthful, smooth, round, clean, lean, relaxed, symmetrical, well-defined, good-postured body is going to be considered more beautiful than, well, mine. Industrial designers know that if you bottled tap water and sold it, the prettier bottle would sell more than the ugly one. So.

But not to put too fine an edge on it. The essential response to these women is not exactly aesthetic.

At eleven, I can't say that I knew for certain precisely what went on between men and women—literally, what went where, or why it went where it went when it did in the first place—but I knew that the bunnies appealed to me, to the extent that I felt compelled to actually rub the pictures of them, as if they were three-dimensional. I'd wager all eleven-year-old boys rub the pictures. I knew that I wanted to kiss the models, squeeze them like Charmin, take baths with them, and at night, I'd pretend my pillow was one. My response was sexual before I knew what sex was.

The photographs still come to life for me, in my imagination, as fantasy fodder. Now I know what goes where, and my fantasies are correspondingly more inspired. The pulse picks up, the eyes widen. They show blue movies to gorillas when they want to get them to mate; the response is that innate. Me and the bunnies do it in elevators, freight trains, on trampolines, and have incredible, lusty, athletic, deafening, furniture-smashing multiple-orgasmic sex, for hours and hours (about five to ten seconds in actual time).

I do not expect the real women I know to look like bunnies. After all, the relationship to the centerfold is imaginary, the appeal of voyeurism the safety of detachment. Imaginary relationships only hurt you if you confuse them with real ones. Ideal means exactly that. My definition of what an ideal *real* person would be is quite different from what *Playboy* offers, one definition of ideal youthful feminine beauty, to be embraced or not. While every man wants the most beautiful lover he can get (and don't women, too?), I don't personally know too many guys who compare the real women they meet to these fantasy models, not any more than they might seriously bank on winning the lottery or hitting a home run in the World Series. We may pine and sigh and look at pictures, daydream, and imagine, but that's usually as far as it can go. Women's romance novels offer, as fantasy fodder, dark brooding lairds and swarthy types on big powerful horses. I know women who feel (legitimately) that they've been raised and taught to be self-conscious about their looks and who resent feeling they're being compared to *Playboy* bunnies, that they should look that way since that's the ideal. I don't know men who feel they have to be dark brooding lairds.

Since we don't *identify* with a woman's resentment at being compared to an ideal, too often we dismiss it, wonder what the fuss is about. Only a gender in a position of power could do that.

It's difficult to know what political position to take. I am for women's equality, but I am against the suppression of sexual information, and I'm not ready to say all erotic imagery should be removed from all our books, movies, or magazines. The thinking of the New Right (kind of an oxymoron) would have it that sexuality is not to be depicted or enjoyed. Maybe it can be enjoyed a little, but only if you're married. The rest of us are to remain numb from the neck down. Sex is *supposed* to be fun—if it weren't, no one would do it, and then there would only be a few thousand people on earth, *all perverts*. The New Right believes that the less information we give our children about sex, the more sensibly they'll behave, that you can prevent teenage pregnancy by limiting teenagers' access to contraceptives, which is like saying the less water you throw on a fire, the sooner it will go out. The Meese Commission Report on Pornography, a document which has been widely discredited by most people with any brains at all (for one example, two men said to operate a major porn ring out of Allentown, Pennsylvania, by the report, had in fact been dead for years) suggested that since many rapists read porn, pornography leads to violence. If that were true, then would this not also be true wherever pornography exists? There's hardly any violence in Sweden, Japan, or Holland, and I saw things openly displayed in shop windows in Amsterdam that would make Hugh Hefner blush. We are an extremely violent country, and some violence is sexual. We're a country with a unique panoply of sexual hang-ups, repressions, and hypocrisies, to the point where, as comedian Jay Leno points out, we use sex in ads to sell everything from toasters to vacations, but when we make commercials for condoms, the ad men fill the television screen with fields of wheat blowing in the breeze and ocean waves crashing on the shore. It seems far too simple to say that pornography causes violence and may just be a way for conservative investigators to avoid asking themselves what causes pornography.

There are, in fact, countries with very little pornography, but it's hard to think of any pornography-free country in the world where any free woman would want to live. China, where they practice infanticide on girl babies? Saudi Arabia, where any part of a woman's body that's not covered is removed in a public amputation with a scimitar? (Okay, I'm wildly exaggerating.) I'm not a world traveler, so I don't know—maybe there is a place pure and holy, some tropical island culture where sexual innocence is never lost. Realistically, here in the land of the First Amendment, there will be porn, and while much of it is disgusting and should be controlled, a magazine like *Playboy* doesn't bother me nearly as much as something like the Miss America Pageant, which hypocritically denies any intent to excite men or make objects of women, when in fact it does only that. It's as close as we come these days to sacrificing virgins.

There will always be lines drawn, beyond which an individual feels uncomfortable venturing, varying from the supreme prude who can't even watch Vanna White turn letters without hyperventilating, to the complete pig who buys pictures beyond description in brown paper bags from anonymous P.O. boxes in Brazil. *Playboy* falls, for many men, into a category describing something both taboo and yet acceptable, it's perusal naughty but innocent. Maybe men who know better *and* read *Playboy* are reliving the innocence of youth, when we first picked up a *Playboy* and were amazed, aroused, tempted, and endangered. Every time Victor Peabody caught us and threw us out the drugstore door, telling us we should be ashamed of ourselves, all we could think was, If this is shame we're feeling, give us more. It's low-minded, but that's part of all of us.

What Men Really Do
at Stag Parties

■

I could suffer severe penalties for revealing to women what actually happens at a "stag" party, or prenuptial bachelor party. One of the final things that occurs at stag parties, after we do the Stag Dance, but before we sing the Stag Anthem, is taking the Pledge of Stag Secrecy, in which we promise never to tell women about "this thing of ours," on pain of having our *spleff maen whithress chlaenn,* which is ancient Druid for something too horrible to translate, but believe me, it hurts.

Women think bachelor parties are a lot of fun, but in truth they are harrowing ordeals, mixing high jinks (like getting the groom drunk and putting him on a plane one way to Nasal, Wyoming) with debauchery and low-level alcohol poisoning. All of this is meant to create an evening so obnoxious that the groom will never think twice about going back to what he was before the party. It is a ceremonial rite of passage, a cleansing away of the lusty and the profane, in order to prepare for the spiritual and sacred. To put it another way, you're supposed to get your yah-yahs out, once and for all. Of course, in real life, no sooner do you get your yah-yahs out than new replacement yah-yahs start to grow. It's the thought that counts.

The night of the party, the groom's buddies pitch in and buy enough beer to get everybody wiener-faced. Someone, usually the guy with the loudest mouth, arranges for provocative entertainment. The summer after high school, I attended a stag party where three strippers were hired to gyrate, one on the coffee table, one on the dining room table, one on the stairway landing, while forty or fifty drooling eighteen-year-olds chain-smoked Camels or Luckies and tucked dollar bills into their garters. The dancers' garters, I mean. These days, X-rated videotapes have no doubt replaced strippers in many instances. The gist is the same. This is the last time the groom can legitimately celebrate the joys of unbridled carnal rapacity, his last chance to crow and strut.

On another level, the stag party is supposed to be a kind of test of the groom's commitment. While the groom is allowed to enjoy the dancing skills of a stripteaser or two, when it's midnight and the dancers head upstairs (if and when they do, though I've never been to one where they actually did), a man who's ready for marriage is supposed to resist the urge to follow them. In my experience, it's all talk, symbolic display behavior. What kind of a jerk would screw a hooker on his wedding night? He publicly puts to rest his wolfish ways, in front of all his peers. It's almost tribal. At this point, most grooms are so plastered that they couldn't do anything anyway, another unacknowledged reason for serving alcohol.

The bridegroom is tested in ways other than by the temptations of the flesh. My friends and I, whenever one of us pairs off, traditionally play poker, acting out with cards and dice the temptations of greed and vice, while raking the pot to pay for the booze and the movies. At one stag party I attended, we played craps, but it was an unusual bachelor party because the bridesmaids showed up, and in fact, the maid of honor took fifty clams off the best man. It is the job of the groom's friends to tell him horror stories of married life, to remind him of ex-girlfriends who still carry torches for him, and finally, just ask him flat out if he knows what the hell he's doing. They'll remind him of other times when he thought he knew what he was doing, like when he bought the 1965 MG for $1,000 and it dropped its transmission the first time out on the highway.

Usually when the party's over, everyone goes out to an all-night diner. Over coffee, tired and calmer, the groom's friends tell him they think he's doing the right thing and wish him luck. They reminisce, just one more time, about the good times everybody had together when they were all young and free. They usually conclude that being older, and married, is better. What else are you going to tell a guy who is about to get married?

The evening ends with the only true stag secret I'll actually reveal: the Stag Handshake. Standing around the parking lot at the all-night diner, the men line up to shake the groom's hand. They grab it firmly, like any ordinary handshake, but then they give it one extra little squeeze, as if to say that, this time, they really mean it. You want the groom to know that he was your friend before the wedding, and he'll be your friend afterward. You want him to know that you think his getting married is a big deal, because, after all the foolishness is over, it really is.

Romance and the Road

·

Men and cars. Men in cars. Men under cars. Men talking cars, racing cars, washing cars, waxing cars, painting cars, swapping cars, salvaging cars. Do men love cars? My friend Arlene told me she was parked in her high school boyfriend Craig's Corvette when he told her there was another woman, and he couldn't afford to keep them both. When she asked, tearfully, who the other woman was, he said, "You're sitting in her."

Craig was a motorhead's motorhead, with oil in his veins and whitewall feet, but even so, women may well wonder what it is with men and their cars. Why do we tinker with, read about, disassemble, reassemble, dwell upon, ooh and/or ahhh at, and in general love them so much? Why do we think about them almost as much as we think about sex?

In a way, thinking about cars *is* thinking about sex.

The passion starts early on, and as we grow, both boys and girls develop a Pavlovian response to the automobile not unlike my old friend Ray's coonhound, which used to have spastic fits and fling itself repeatedly into the front door until unconscious when you so much as jangled the car keys at it. Cars are exciting. They take us places like Grandma's, where she gives us candy. "Going for a ride" (unless you're a gangster's kid, in which case it's what happens to you if you don't finish your peas) becomes synonymous with promise, good times, special food.

Then we begin to differentiate. While girls are using dolls to

21

play out scenarios containing real-life emotions and problems, boys are studying the physical relationships between objects, like how many times can you smash a plastic toy car into a wooden chair leg before one or the other breaks. Motorized vehicles are among the first and most glamorous objects in a boy's life. Two of the first words I spoke were "cow" (car) and "twuck" (truck).

Boys watch millions of car commercials on television every day, showing us who we're going to be when we grow up and own cars— happy smiling sexy windblown people going places. Between the commercials, we see TV shows with chase scene after chase scene, giving us a pretty good idea how we think we're going to drive. Knowing this, adults begin, about when we're in high school, to try to scare the bejeebers out of us by making us take driver's ed classes, in which a man who hasn't changed his tie in twenty years runs movies like *Death on the Highway* or *The Last Prom* where they show you actual charred bodies. We learned our lesson well. Never, under any circumstances, be in a driver's ed movie. I didn't care though. Not about the danger, or the financial responsibilities, or the cost in human lives getting my license was going to exact. I'd been riding around with older friends who already had their licenses, and I knew what having one meant:

Freedom.

The first thing a boy thinks, *alone* behind the wheel, his brand-new driver's license still warm from the laminator, is: "I could go to California if I want to." (Unless he's already in California.) The empowerment is immediate—for the first time in his life, he can go wherever he wants, whenever he feels like it. When I got my permit, gas was thirty-two cents a gallon, about what a school lunch cost. Cut lunch for a week and I had enough gas to go to Wisconsin! Then the boy realizes, it's not just a method of transportation— it's his first private, personal space. Your parents can walk into your bedroom, and the principal can have your school locker opened and inspected at will, but nobody can violate the privacy of your car or know what you do in it. Keep the smokes low when you pass a cop and you've got it made. You don't have to be Albert Einstein to guess what a teenage boy is going to do with his own first private personal space, when it's given to him—he's going to smoke, drink, and make out with girls in it.

I remember adolescence as little more than chronic bouts of ineluctable boredom aggravated by unrequitable sexual longings and imaginings relieved only by nightly cruises around town, and I can honestly say that as best as I can remember, I did not go to bed once, from somewhere around 1969 to the time I left home, without having gotten out of the house to cruise first. The car was the only way I could get well. I found hope in a simple assumption: that nothing good is going to come to you if you stay where you are, so you have to keep moving.

I cruised the lakes of Minneapolis, looking for chicks, and I had a special route I took every night before heading back to the garage, a winding journey that took me past the houses of all the girls I had the hots for, because there was always the chance I'd see one through her bedroom window, or even get to honk casually at one out raking the lawn, say, at midnight. My route never doubled back past the same house twice, lest someone see me and surmise I was driving by on purpose. It had to look accidental. I didn't want these girls to think I *liked* them.

We hung out at a drive-in actually called Porky's (with drawings of Porky Pig on the menu), hoping to score up a carload of bachelorettes. One summer, my friend Schmitty and I snuck out our bedroom windows at two in the morning, sometimes three or four times a week, rolled his mother's car into the street, and drove off into the night, for wherever we "heard" girls were (inventing fictions, of course, since the only place girls were was where we weren't—in bed). It wasn't so much the octane in the gas as the hormones flooding our nervous systems that drove us on. They had to be somewhere, convertibles teeming with blondes, vans stuffed full of cheerleaders, buses o' babes. There had to be.

Keep this sort of thing up for four or five years, and eventually you reach the logical counterpart to cruising, which is *parking*. I'd guess more sexual firsts happen in cars in America than anywhere else, including basement rec-room couches when the folks are out. Parking is a thrill that is only increased by the imminent possibility that cops are going to pull up any minute and catch you with your windows fogged. It is also one of the places boys learn in practice what their psychology classes have been telling them in theory, that adolescent girls are more mature than boys. To compensate, boys try to impress girls by knowing about cars, on the admittedly shaky premise that knowledge and expertise about the workings of an internal combustion engine implies or connotes a similar command of the machinations of the human heart. This, any girl who's ever escaped from a Chevelle SS after an hour of clumsy groping with nothing but the imprint of a door handle permanently embossed into the back of her neck to show for it, knows just isn't true.

When we're older, and the hormones have simmered down, the passion for automobiles remains. A man never grows out of this love. He grows *into* it. He discovers a car's unlimited uses. He can go to the beach in it, take it to a country auction, stop for roadside picnic lunches, or follow a long late-night stretch of empty Montana road, listening to a Dodgers game in extra innings, while the most important person in the world sleeps with her head in his lap, and he runs his fingers through her hair. Romance is the road.

A car is usually the second biggest thing a man can buy, after a house. His prestige and his sense of identity are more on the line with a car than with a house, since more people will see his car. It's a reflection of his ego, symbolic of his self-image. A man thinks of himself as a Volvo man, a Dodge Dart man, an old station-wagon man, and he sees all the cars he's ever owned in his life lining up in his memory like a string of lost loves, the one that broke his heart in Cleveland, the one that saved his life in Oregon.

To be fair, for all the guys who put their cars up on pedestals, there are a few who regard their cars like any other appliance. Take the autophobe, the guy who hates cars and doesn't drive, or if he drives, regards his car like a distance processor to go with his food and word processors. A real curable romantic. I suppose you can be a valid human being without an automobile, and I grant that it may well be irrational to have an emotional relationship with an inanimate object. Still, anyone who sees cars as mere inanimate objects must have one for a soul as well. The car today is what the raft was to Huck Finn, the horse to Don Quixote or the paladins of yore. I met a paladin of yore once, and he agreed completely.

Not that any man who favors the automobile is automatically better—there are also auto-phonies. Most obvious are the guys with the gold chains and the open shirts who walk into the showroom and ask the dealer, "What do you have in a two-door phallic substitute?" and go $50,000 in debt for a Porsche that can go nearly four times faster than it's legal or considerate to go. I knew a guy, Wilson, who drove a luxury Audi he was immensely proud of, but knew next to nothing about. He'd bring it back to the dealer twice a year to have it vacuumed, washed, and waxed, forking over piles of dough for cosmetics. He'd carry his removable tape deck under his arm the way Marilyn Monroe carried an intellectual magazine under hers—to be seen with it.

A true autophile appreciates the symbolic value of his car, its form, but also its function. He wants to get involved with it, and understand it, take care of it. If I were to rank the guys I know in order of trustworthiness or dependability, the car nuts among them would all be near the top. Maybe it's because they're the ones I call when I've popped a timing chain by the side of the road, or when I'm into a repair job and find myself over my head. They are simply solid and reliable. They are patient, and know how to work through problems one step at a time and not get discouraged. To be fair, they'd also all wind up near the bottom of my luck-with-women list, maybe because they found solace on dateless Friday high school nights under GTOs, pulling transmissions apart instead of venturing out into the mysterious and confusing world of romance. Still, they're probably the guys I'd be most likely to set my sisters up with. Over the objections of my brothers-in-law, no doubt, but you can't please everybody.

The way a man drives is revealing as well. Suppose you get in the car with a man, on your first date, and he pulls away from the curb. Suddenly you realize, you're not going to make it back alive.

Driving can be the elixir that turns a Dr. Jekyll into a Mr. Hyde, almost a truth serum. My theory is that the physical act of driving, using all one's senses, visually measuring vector and velocity from passing fence posts, listening for changes in engine hum, smelling for gas, feeling the centrifugal force of a turn in your inner ear and the way your center of gravity gets pulled from side to side, involves enough of one's active consciousness to free a suppressed part of the psyche, affecting a temporary personality change.

My friend Jeff, for example, wouldn't ordinarily pick a fight with anyone. He's basically a peaceful, gentle man, but he'll cuss like a sailor at anybody who passes him on the right. Once we even chased a guy for three blocks because he cut in front of us, until I convinced Jeff of the larger picture—namely, that the guy was four times larger than us and would beat us into comas with his tire iron if we actually caught him.

Driving can also reveal a man's best side. Men who are ordinarily wired and anxious can become serene and meditative when they drive. On a long trip, I'll compose symphonies, develop nine-step plans to lasting world peace, but five minutes after I stop the car, I forget all of it. For a while, though, I was a better person.

Men who have soft spots for cars are likely to have them as well for women who like cars. I'm usually impressed when I meet a woman who knows something about engines, takes the initiative to find out how things work. Working on cars together is a form of male bonding that can make a Harvard Law School professor pals with his high school–dropout mechanic, and there's no reason it couldn't bond men to women as well. I wouldn't even mind taking a night course in car mechanics with my girlfriend, though I'm sure not everyone will think that's terribly romantic.

There are plenty of other romantic things men and women can do together, in and around cars, apart from fogging up the windows. You can wash the car together, a great American summer Saturday afternoon pastime, along with visiting state fairs or zoos. You can go to drive-in movies, a former great American Saturday night pastime. The movies shown are usually terrible, but as thinly veiled excuses to make out, watching *Kung Fu Cheerleaders* won't kill you. You can take a cross-country trip, sticking to the blue highways. If you don't want to go too far, just cruise for burgers in the dying light of a hot summer night. You can still go parking, though after you reach a certain age, say twenty-three or so, try to find a spot where the kids won't point at you and laugh.

I had more than a small soft spot for one woman because of something that happened involving my last beat-up old station wagon, a 1977 Subaru whose four-wheel drive I'd been boasting about for months, how we could drive to the North Pole or climb redwood trees with it if we wanted to. Unfortunately one cold, wintry night on an empty stretch of interstate, the car began to gradually lose power, from what I guessed was a blown head gasket, until we were dead on the shoulder of the road.

"Four-wheel drive, Pete?" she said.

"Very funny," I said. I grabbed the flashlight and got out to have a look under the hood.

"What do you think it is?" she said. I looked up to realize she was standing next to me, looking into the engine too, and I thought, What are you doing here? Most people would wait in the car where it's warm. In that moment, I saw that her instinct would be to stand beside me, even through something like a roadside break-down. If that were true of *minor* crises—what promise it held for major ones! I felt moved, and suddenly much fonder of her. We kissed, in the freezing wind at the side of the highway. When we got back in, swear to God, I tried the ignition one more time; it started up fine and took us all the way home. I knew love was powerful and mysterious, but I didn't know it could fix blown head gaskets.

Shakespeare once wrote, "The course of true love never did run smooth." My Subaru never did run smooth either, but it got me where I wanted to be. Six months after the roadside incident, I moved in with that woman, to a small town in Massachusetts where it was obvious from the start that one could get by quite well without a car, and I think the Subaru knew it. It got me here, took one look around, and gave up the ghost. I could have put it on an artificial life-support system and kept it alive for a few more years, but I decided to pull the plugs and let it rest in peace. It is driving today down some heavenly blacktop, whispering like a new fan, reaching tremendous speeds and getting incredible mileage, gone but not forgotten.

Blondes

■

I have no desire to offend or slight, and would say at the outset that the woman I love has ravishing auburn hair evocative of sunsets in the redwoods, expensive chocolates, and chestnuts roasting on an open fire—it catches light like a prom ball, and I love to run my fingers through it. I have women friends with shiny ebon manes black as wrought iron, I'm on a first-name basis with as many redheads as any man could hope to shake a stick at, and I wouldn't want any of them to change a hair for me. Not if they care for me. *But* . . . there is, all the same, an enduring (or irrepressible) mystique about *blondes*. There is a popular mythology, or at least a body of clichés surrounding them, that won't go away—that they have more fun, that gentlemen prefer them, that they find men who write for women's magazines irresistible, or that they are somehow superior to other women, at least in the eyes of some men. It's a mythology as alive now as ever.

In the sixties, we asked, "Does she or doesn't she?" and only her hairdresser knew for sure. In the eighties, the question seems to have been rendered moot by a public attitude that falls somewhere between Fernando's (Billy Crystal's) "it's better to look good than to feel good" and Norman Mailer's declaration that "any woman who dyes her hair blond *is* a real blonde." Now, whether she does or doesn't doesn't matter, and only a hairdresser would think to ask.

I think the revival started with the 1980 Olympic men's hockey team, turning things around in their victory over the Russians and encouraging us all to "go for the gold," after which some women took that advice to heart, or at least let it go to their heads. It's been a feel-good let-yourself-flash sort of decade. So we have Cybill Shepherd, Jessica Lange, and Kim Bassinger gracing our silver screens, Belinda Carlyle and Debbie Harry and the indomitable Madonna tossing their yellow locks off their bare shoulders inside our MTVs, and everybody's mailman is writing a book about the real Marilyn Monroe and the time she hunted water buffalo in the nude with Hemingway on Frank Sinatra's private game preserve. Whoever's idea it was, being blond is making a comeback. Don't hold your breath, waiting for men to voice any complaints.

Auricomophilia (love of blondes) has a long history. The first recorded mention of it can be found in Ovid's *Metamorphoses*, in the story of Jason and the Argonauts, who cruised the Aegean Sea looking for "golden fleece." Predating that may be the story of Perseus and the Gorgon, a woman from whose head protruded a hundred snakes, though some scholars believe that to be a mistranslation, and that she actually had hair with a hundred *streaks*, referring to the crude application of the primitive peroxides popular among the mythological figures of the era.

In the Middle Ages, the siren of the folktale was medieval Europe's preeminent blonde, Goldielocks. Young girls may have dreamed of being Cinderella, but Goldielocks was their down-to-earth role model, more so even than her chief rival, Rapunzel, of whom Goldie once said at a cocktail party, "Yeah, sure, fifteen feet of blond hair, but don't forget, the first twelve inches are pure black roots." Fairy godmothers had blond hair, while witches and evil queens had hair as black as their black, black hearts.

In modern America, the glorification of the blonde is largely a media-orchestrated phenomenon. As soon as they invented a way to project someone's photograph fifty times its actual size on the motion picture screen, they invented a blond sex symbol who was about fifty times her actual size off the screen as well as on, in the person of Mae West. She set the standard and was exactly the type of woman "gentlemen" weren't supposed to prefer. Her success begat innumerable imitators, from Jean Harlow to Veronica Lake, women introduced to us as sex symbols who batted bedroom eyes and seemed to smile dirty all the time. It's hard to say whether Hollywood gave American men what they wanted or told them what to want, but one way or the other, the color for our sex goddesses' hair was designated blond, maybe only because in the days of black-and-white film, they didn't have much of a palate to choose from—the blondes were the ones who stuck out in a crowd. Eventually even good girls could be blond (or perhaps had to be, to sell tickets at the box office), and Hollywood gave us Donna Reed, June Allyson, Grace Kelly, and that embodiment of girl-next-door virtue herself, Doris Day. I was never real clear on exactly why all those leading men were so intent on seducing her, but if it wasn't her hair, then what else could it have been?

In part, it's that tension between vamp and virgin that gives the blonde her mystique, the belief that there must have been some wholesome part to Mae West, though she hid it well, and that there had to be some evil in Doris Day, who hid it even better. It's a color that appeals to both sides of a man's nature, the desire to save and protect as well as to defile and corrupt. The cognitive dissonance can be engaging. A man's reaction to any blonde met at a party or in a club is probably informed by the idea of the collective blonde he carries around in his imagination, shaped from an amalgam of the blond images he grew up with. He wonders who she is, wants to explore her, lured in by the symbolism of her hair.

For me, as a typical kid weaned on TV and Kool-Aid, the good blondes of my boyhood were Hayley Mills, Hoss Cartwright's fiancée whatever-her-name-was on "Bonanza," Samantha on "Bewitched," and an assortment of mothers: Beaver's mom, Dennis the Menace's mom, Donna Reed. The evil blondes were Tuesday Weld from "Dobie Gillis"; Joey Heatherton, though I couldn't tell you where I ever saw her; and all the platinum-tressed home wreckers, murderesses, and gangsters' molls who populated shows like "Perry Mason" or "Peter Gunn"—pretty much second-class bimbos told to go wait in cars or take hikes while tough guys talked over big heists, but dangerous in their own right, liable to poison anybody at all for nothing more than a mink stole or a ride in a Cadillac. I learned to expect something exciting to happen whenever a blond actress appeared. She was the brandished pistol in the first act, who I knew would be used before the final curtain.

I think this all has something to do with why I felt so attracted to the first blonde I ever met in my real life, literally the girl next door, whose name was Mary Johnson. I was four, and she was at least five, because she'd loan me her bicycle, which didn't even have training wheels on it. Her hair was white as the driven snow, straight with bangs, and I loved her with all my heart. Off and on. One day she told me she had to go take a bath. Not knowing I was doing anything wrong, I decided to haul a stepladder over to their bathroom window and surprise her, just sort of check her out, I suppose. I know I was wearing corduroy pants with an elastic belt, because I remember how strange it felt when my mother grabbed me by the waistband and pulled me down off the ladder, just as I'd nearly reached the top step. It's probably why I'm frightened to climb up on them today. Not blondes—ladders.

Blondes are also valued, apart from what we're told about them in movies and television, for their scarcity, gold being a color prized in both hair and metal. Most of the blond women I know who've traveled in Latin countries where blondes are as rare as snowmobile dealers have stories to tell of situations when they found their blondness, well, grossly overvalued, preferred but not by gentlemen. A man might be attracted to a blonde just because he's never kissed one and wonders what it's like.

To be honest, I'm not sure. Growing up in Minneapolis and being of 100 percent Norwegian heritage disqualifies me, I think, from talking about scarcity. Though my own hair was almost snow white until I was old enough to peep on Mary Johnson, it is now the color of strong coffee with maybe half a creamer in it, definitely *brown*, but even so I've been told *I'm* blond, in places I've lived like Rhode Island or Arizona, where the majority of the population is black-haired. I tell people they don't know blond. I know blond. I come from the land of Jessica Lange and Cybill Shepherd. Six out of my first ten girlfriends were blondes. In fact, two of them were

Jessica Lange and Cybill Shepherd. Yeah, that's the ticket. At any rate, knockout blondes are a dime a dozen in Minnesota. Sometimes when I meet a blonde, and she happens to be a fellow Scandinavian, I think more about how pleased my old Norwegian grandmother would be if I married her than about anything sexual. Not *precisely* the take most guys have, I'm sure. But I do like blondes, and I think I've known enough of them to say why.

It's because they know they're blond. I don't mean they look in the mirror and see it—they wake up feeling in their hearts that they *are* it. It's not ego or self-centeredness, necessarily, so much as a well-defined sense of themselves, because all their lives, their blond hair has been the first thing people have commented on. "Such lovely blond hair—you'll sure break the boys' hearts in a few years." "Hey, blondie . . . hey, Goldielocks. . . ." They get complimented. They get attention. Sometimes it screws them up, but sometimes it frees them from worrying about their looks, or gives them a sense of power, confidence.

A writer friend of mine, a few years ago, dyed her hair blond for thirty days and wrote an article about it. She found out pretty much the same thing. People started looking twice at her, though she was fairly golden-haired to begin with. She felt more present in a roomful of people, more able to walk into a party and get noticed. Heads turned. People smiled at her. She knew it was based on a false premise, but her self-image improved anyway. It simply *was* more fun. The old slogan proved true. If it wasn't the hair, then what else could it have been?

If gentlemen still prefer blondes, in the final analysis they do so because they enjoy the spirit of blondness, the versatility of it. It's fresh, pure, and wholesome, athletic, all-American; it's sexy, nasty, a flirt flag, a bold stroke made by a bold person when it's dyed; it's flaxen, dishwater, platinum, honey, bleached or frosted, straw or saffron, lemon or butter or canary yellow, champagne or sand, chrome or strawberry, but as Rapunzel might have said, as long as it's blond, even if it's not as blond as it's long, gentlemen will prefer it.

Waitresses

■

If I were rich, I'd like to be one of those surprise philanthropists the newspapers are always reporting about, the apparent bag-lady who leaves a million bucks to the local animal shelter, or the self-made refrigerator-magnet magnate who gives a new wing to the vocational high school that flunked him. I know who I'd give my money to, though they have no national foundation or pension fund to put my fortune in. I'd get a million dollars in nickels, dimes, and quarters, and leave it all on the tables of all the restaurants in America.

My love for waitresses goes back to my earliest memories. A kid, a puppy, a baby duck—it doesn't matter—will love whoever brings it food. The first person to do that is his mother, but the second person in a kid's life to do that is usually a waitress, sort of a backup free-lance mother. I'd be sitting in my booster seat, and some friendly waitress would come over, ruffle my curly yellow hair, and say, "What a good boy—you finished it all," and I'd be completely taken in, though in fact they probably hated my little guts, since at that age my preferred way to clean my plate was to throw whatever I found on it across the room.

My appreciation soared when I got a job tending bar in a restaurant. I saw a report in a magazine that said waiting on tables topped air-traffic control for job-related stress, and it didn't surprise me. When you're a bartender, you at least have a substantial slab of wood between you and *them*, and you can use it as a barricade, turn your back to wipe a counter, and poof, magic, no more *them*. Wait on tables, and you're out among *them*. You can run, but you can't hide. If you've ever seen dogs snarl at each other over a bone, you know that in the face of hunger, good manners go right out the window. Diners want their food their way, and they want it ten minutes ago, and they don't care if they're snappish or rude about asking for it because they're hungry. Who suffers? Not the cooks, dishwashers, busboys, bartenders, none of the people who may be equally to blame if the food really is unacceptably slow in coming, and often they're doing the best they can too. The waitresses suffer, women on the short end of the stick anyway for having to wait tables in the first place, but it was all the work they could find. Becoming a waitress is not exactly a career move, but the money can be good. It pays the rent. In fact, it would be a great job, if it weren't for *them*.

Waitresses bear up. It's ennobling. Some turn sour and glum, slouching from table to table in joyless despair, but most seem to know that this is how life is for everyone, if only temporarily, and go stoically about their business. All eventually come to the bartender, sooner or later, with an imploring look in their eyes universal to waitresses everywhere. It's a look that says, "Please, give me a shot of whiskey, now, or I'll die." Who wouldn't have sympathy?

Some waitresses even find *pleasure* in the job. I worked with a woman we called "Little Deb," to distinguish her from "Big Deb," who was bigger. Little Deb was five-foot-one, had curly brown hair and an impish grin. She smiled all the time, chatted with the customers, joked, laughed, flirted. She might even have had too much fun. More people walked out on her without paying than on any other waitress or waiter in the place, because she didn't pay close enough attention and let them, and because she was short and they thought she wouldn't see them do it. The boss made the floor personnel pay the checks themselves on walkouts. One night, a guy in a wheelchair *rolled away* on Little Deb. She ran after him, full of fire and tears, but she was too late. He'd vanished into the night. Somehow, she was her cheerful self the next day. It's a job that tests the spirit. As Nietzsche said, "That which doesn't kill me makes me stronger."

They all get even too, one way or another, in their fantasies if nowhere else. The things waitresses say about what they'd like to do to *them*, when *they* can't hear, would make a sailor blush. Waitresses have memories like elephants. If you don't believe me, short-tip a waitress in January, go back in June, and see how long it takes her to find her way to your table. A friend worked in a place where they had an obnoxious customer—call him Joe—who always asked if the coffee was fresh. "I don't want it if it's been on the burner," he would always say, or he'd send it back, complaining, "I wouldn't drink that dreck if you paid me—I'll just wait for a fresh pot." One day a waitress named Ruth couldn't take it any-more. She found a pot with a half inch of coffee in it, took it to the kitchen, and boiled it for ten minutes, until it was black as tar. "Here ya go, Joe," she said, "a nice fresh pot." He took a sip and sighed with delight. "Ahhhh," he said, "now *that's* good coffee."

I'm biased. They're the first people I meet when I move to a new town. I write in restaurants, and sometimes I see more of my waitress friends than I do of my girlfriend. I never treat eating in a restaurant like the last privilege of the ruling class, where anybody can plunk down a few bucks and pretend they have servants. I think of waitresses as working stiffs, laboring at a task far more difficult than it looks. I try to show understanding and compassion. They work hard and tolerate much. Be good to your waitresses. I'll never have a million dollars to give them. You'll have to do it for me.

Do Men Kiss and Tell?

■

"So you're seeing Sam," I said to my friend Wanda.

"What?" she said. She was shocked and appalled. "What did he tell you?"

"Nothing, really," I said, coming to Sam's defense. "Just that you two spent a night together." Actually, Sam had added, "I'm telling you, Pete, if it could be like that all the time, I don't know—this could be the real thing."

"That little weasel," Wanda said. "If he said anything at all, I'll kick his face in."

I gathered that Sam had broken a confidence. But Sam wasn't the kind of guy who talked about every new sexual escapade as if it were a fresh notch in a gun handle. He was just excited—something terrific had happened to him, and he wanted me to know. To Wanda, Sam had kissed and told.

"Sounds to me like there's been a failure to communicate," I said.

"Sounds to me like someone has communicated altogether too well," Wanda said.

I wouldn't say it's common, but men do occasionally kiss and tell. They do it for a number of reasons—some good, some bad. There are men who need to make it known that they score a lot, hoping to join Dons Juan and Johnson on the list of famous ladies' men. Obviously men who boast about their exploits would do so out of insecurity, seeking the approving nods or chortles of their comrades to assuage the doubt. The traditional image of the insensitive jerk who kisses and tells is that of the schmoe in the locker room, entertaining his buddies with the graphic details of his date the night before, complete with name, place, sound effects, and visual aids. I know a guy named Alex who needs little prompting.

"Hi, Alex," I'll say, "how are you?"

"Oh man," he'll say, "this last month has been absolutely incredible, really, I tell you—I went out to Malibu with Jerry and his girlfriend Rita, and like right away I met this beautiful young girl from San Francisco, Peter, we're like rabbits, man—she had to be the sexiest thing I'd ever seen, but then, get this, one day Jerry goes into town to get a newspaper, and Rita and I are lying on the beach and all of a sudden, I feel this hand on my leg, and it's Rita, so right then and there, man, on the beach—amazing!"

"I'm fine too, thanks," I say.

He'll lift his shirt to show the scratch marks when there are any. If you want to avoid people like Alex, I would guess you'd want to shun men who boast about other things. A man who somehow lets it drop within five minutes of the moment you first meet him what big-shot people he knows or how much money he makes a year probably tells his friends how many dates he makes a year.

Alex is, however, the only guy I know who easily comes to mind as the type to kiss and tell on purpose. More men may do so by accident. A lot of guys wouldn't blab if the women they kissed told them not to, but men don't always have particularly keen instincts about what's going to embarrass women. As a rule, men would think, It doesn't embarrass me, so why should it embarrass her? The golden rule, in this case, is a thoroughly flawed tenet. If you tell men, "This is just between you and me," or, "Repeat this and I'll kick your face in," we'll usually get the point. Don't assume we're like you—it's as wrong as our assuming you're like us.

There are times, however, when it may actually be to a woman's benefit for a man to kiss and tell. If he's troubled about a relationship, confiding openly in a best buddy can help him straighten out problems he couldn't solve on his own. My friend Rick told me he'd failed in bed one night. He was worried that it meant he didn't love his girlfriend anymore. We talked it through, to the conclusion that it could easily happen even when you're in love. Rick's girlfriend certainly wouldn't have wanted their private life made public, even if it went no further than me, but if Rick hadn't talked to someone about it, he might have ended the relationship privately and prematurely.

Men *should* talk to each other. I'm not sure why we don't. My friends and I never talk about it. Merely trying to explain the silence between men as a simple expression of basic competitiveness, or of homophobia (the fear of being overpowered by the pleasure of being intimate with another man), or of both, still doesn't seem to go far enough. Men take care of our need for intimacy metaphorically, maybe to an extent women don't fully appreciate. Once removed, but then we're the ones making the implicit agreement to remove it once. If it appears silly, to women, when men argue at absurdly great lengths over who threw the pitch (and exactly what kind of pitch was it?) that Mickey Mantle hit out of the stadium against the Washington Senators, or why German automotive engineering is superior to Japanese, it *feels good* to men. We help each other feel good. It's when the talk gets personal that we clam up, or at least guard ourselves, personal as far as disclosing fears or doubts, or describing innermost emotions. We take after our fathers, the figure who felt obligated to be the strong one in the family, just because his was the loudest voice or the firmest spanking hand, the power that could bring order to the chaos a family of howling kiddies can be. My own father was fairly taciturn or stoic, not really big on dwelling on weaknesses or over-examining them, and I inherited some of that. At least I try to think through things on my own, not defer to the authority of others. When I talk to my friends, I'm glad to hear it when they describe reaching conclusions I've already reached independently or confirm suspicions I've been having, but I'd rather not ask for help or advice when I can avoid it, because it means more to me to solve my problems alone. And as far as kissing and telling goes—it's nobody's business. I put more in writing than I pass along in gossip. When I consult male friends about romantic problems, I pretend it's for an article I'm working on.

With one exception. I might kiss and tell simply because I can't contain my feelings, just as when Sam told me about him and Wanda. When I fall in love, it's awfully hard to keep the news to myself. Wanda and Sam became a real solid couple, and I like to think I helped. Then their relationship dissolved, an event which I had nothing to do with, but better to have kissed and told than never to have kissed at all.

Infidelity

•

I guess I've been unfaithful. It was only a kiss, not an affair. And I did it two days before the woman I was living with did it too. Our mutual sinning was more the beginning of the end, symptomatic of a sick situation, than stabs at outside romance to supplement one that mattered. Though we were equally guilty, and I could hardly accuse her or say I didn't understand, the hurt I felt was overwhelming, not to mention that I wasn't entirely proud of myself either. I'd resolved never to be one of "those guys," but I found my resolve unable to withstand the twisted logic of temptation, where opposite desires argued loudly with each other in my conscience.

Statistics suggest there are a lot of "those guys" around. In studies, you get statistics ranging from 50 to 90 percent of all married or otherwise "committed" men. The numbers are so high you could almost argue that unwavering monogamous bonding is an unnatural condition, the question being more "Why not cheat?" than "Why?"

Why men want to cheat is easy. I can second Jimmy Carter's testimony as to having "committed adultery in my heart many times." I experience lust attacks every ten seconds or so, except in spring or when there are actual women around, and then it's more. I'm always having compelling fantasies, a sudden desire for a jug of wine, a loaf of bread, and the supermarket checkout girl who sold them to me. Show me a smile or a leg or a fleeting glimpse of modest bust and bells go off, my response to mating cues, the procreative impulse that got us here. It's not really a question of whether or not I love my girlfriend—she could be superhumanly wonderful and I'd still have a goatish side to me. Men in lust aren't interested in quality. They are drawn to the *new*, the prospect of fresh, unexpected intimacy with a stranger. Where the twisted logic comes in is that love and lust can feel so different that cheating seems a thing separate from and unrelated to the primary relationship. Love is spiritual, abstract, true, deep, lasting, *meaningful*. Lust is here, now, meaningless, fleeting, but urgent.

Here's how the whole thing can start. A man falls in love with woman A, but after the initial glow has worn off, he realizes that women B through Z didn't suddenly become as unappealing to him as he thought they would. There's a popular myth that says this happens. If there were such a thing as an end to want, the rich wouldn't get richer, but they do. It's more like going on a diet, believing you won't be hungry, when in reality, go on a diet and the world suddenly seems mined with chocolate eclairs. The man who has promised himself to be faithful denies the craving, but he can't defeat it or banish it from his thoughts. He settles in with woman A, because he loves her, but he misses having women respond to him sexually, which used to make him feel good about himself, so he flirts.

Then *opportunities* arise. Maybe he turns down opportunities B, C, and D, but woman E has that certain . . . ooh-lah-lah. He can't resist nibbling on the eclair. He thinks of cute words to describe the sin he contemplates. He tells himself it's a fling, not a betrayal, says it's a crush, nothing more. Flesh is weak. He never said he was perfect. Only human. Tired of being strong. It has nothing to do with woman A—he loves her, he knows it. This is different. Just this once. A drink, that's all. What's the harm? Two drinks. A kiss.

Asshole.

That's the twisted logic, the way men who are happy in their relationships, but stray all the same, might justify it. Everyone has urges, from the idea of shoplifting a pencil on a whim to dispatching the neighbor's yappy terrier with a nine-iron (or a seven-, depending on the lie). A man will act on a sexual urge because he *can*. He won't be ostracized. He might even be lionized—hell, Picasso had mistresses, Charlie Chaplin too. He won't get pregnant. He won't get fired. He doesn't have to see getting caught and/or left by his primary other as the end of companionship, since demographically, his chances of starting over are better than hers. Or he thinks, hey, this is America—you can have anything you want in America. A nice tidy affair is just part of life's package. Who thinks this way? Anybody—low-lifes or high-minded moral men succumbing to temptation, liberals, conservatives, priests and schoolteachers—thinking: one more lover, just one, then it will be out of his system.

We were discussing lust once when a buddy said, "Geez, Peter, how many women do you have to sleep with before you learn there's something more important than that?" I thought, Exactly—how many? I wanted a number. Some therapists say secondary affairs can be good for primary relationships, which might be true, if it's the only way a man can learn there is no finite number, no end to the wild oats he can sow if he wants to, except the end he puts to it.

This is the conclusion I've reached, and why I'd rather not cheat. I've been cheated against too, and I know how awful that feels. It's one thing to understand intellectually that we are not objects to be possessed by one another, but it's wholly impossible to believe that in your heart, when you learn the person you love has given him- or herself to someone else. I'm completely inexperienced when it comes to violence, but the rage I felt when Lucy told me she'd kissed someone else verged on the murderous. I didn't want to run into the guy because I was half afraid I'd try to hit him with my car and half afraid I wouldn't. "Carnal knowledge" sounds like such an archaism, but that's what I felt I'd been robbed of—the hard struggle we'd undergone for so long to make the relationship work entitled me, I felt, to the exclusive knowledge of Lucy and all her sexuality, from what it felt like to run my tongue across her teeth in a kiss to the private nonverbal spiritual fusion of lovemaking. This was *our secret*, the only thing we had that no one else could know, and it made us unique. Being cheated on made the whole world seem suddenly so banal, gray, and empty. The weight of the disappointment was crushing. I remember how much it hurt, when the impulse to cheat occurs to me and know I wouldn't wish it on a dog, let alone a loved one. It keeps lust in balance.

Honesty, finally, causes a lot less anxiety, or as Mark Twain put it, "When you tell the truth, you don't have to remember anything." The last time a woman propositioned me (it happens once every five years or so) and I was unavailable, I told her, "Thanks for the compliment, but rules are rules." I felt both a little proud of myself for being strong, and a little relieved at how easy it was. And glad I didn't have to spend any more time thinking about it. I cannot defeat or banish the urge, but I can contain it. It simplifies things to keep lust in the heart, where it belongs.

Growing Up the Hard Way

■

The most obvious differences between men and women are physical. I often wonder if the physical differences don't explain everything else. Would it still be a patriarchal society if women were twice the size and strength of men? Would men be so obsessed with controlling everything if they weren't so repeatedly confronted with a sexual organ that seems to operate or *not* operate with a mind of its own—the penis?

There's an old joke in which a woman is trying to describe to her husband what it feels like to give birth, just how much it hurts. "Pull your lower lip with both hands until you feel pain," she says. He does. "Does that hurt?" He nods. "Now pull it out even farther until it *really* hurts. How's that?" He grimaces in anguish. "Okay, now," she says, "pull it over your head."

I know of no corresponding joke or way to describe what it's like to have a penis. It is a varied experience to say the least. It can be lousy, and it can be wonderful. I will try to be frank. It's a subject men often have difficulty talking about. Beginning with the lousy, then, and working toward the wonderful. . . .

It's two o'clock in the morning. The cat is staring out the window. It's so quiet Jane can hear the diodes flipping in the digital clock. A candle stub drops into the wine bottle holding it, sputters, and goes out. Something has gone wrong. There's a man lying beside her with something that looks like a penis, that's located exactly

45

where penises are supposed to be, but it has failed to act like a penis. She doesn't understand what happened or what he's feeling, and she doesn't know what to say. She wonders if she doesn't turn him on, or if he doesn't love her. She makes a silent vow to watch Phil Donahue more often. She hears Dick sigh heavily.

"It's okay," she says. Easy enough for her to say.

"Yeah, it's great," Dick replies. "I wish I felt this bad all the time."

"No, really," she says. "It's really not a big deal."

"Good word choice," he says.

The question that goes begging is, What's with Dick's dong? Why does it do what it does, and why doesn't it when it doesn't? At one time, it was probably all much easier.

Look at Dick's prehistoric ancestors. It used to be simple, perhaps brutish and ugly, but simple, back when we were uncivilized and unevolved. Somewhere along the line, it got complicated. Some anthropologists say that once we lost our primitive ability to either show or recognize outward signs of sexual readiness, ancient man had to hang around ancient woman and keep his eyes open if he wanted to procreate, instead of taking camping trips whenever he wanted to, evolution favoring Neanderthal-man-on-the-spot. Another theory has it that prehistoric women, faced with migrations or changes in the food supply, found it harder and harder to both raise kids and gather nuts and berries alone, and invented recreational sex as a way of keeping ancient man around to pitch in. The point is that somewhere down the line our sexuality switched from being animal to human, instinctive to voluntary. The Bible dates the origin of sexual self-consciousness roughly around the time Adam and Eve, snacking off the Tree of Knowledge, realized they were buck-naked in the woods and discovered shame. That the end of paradise, figuratively speaking, is dated from this incident is no coincidence. There were Adamite cults in the Middle Ages that tried to rediscover paradise through sexual practices; there are Zen masters today, love communes in California, people still trying to unload the behavioral baggage we carry around.

Physiologically, men's and women's genitals are identical at the zygotic level, the stage before the embryo begins to sexually differentiate. The cells that will form the clitoris on a woman become, in the male with the help of androgen, the head of a man's penis, and mature to hold approximately the same number of nerve endings, though ours are spread out over a greater surface area. It's not the nerve structures so much as the plumbing that makes the big difference.

Between potty training and puberty, a boy knows his penis as nothing more than a terrific squirt gun. When my father used to knock the ashes from his pipe into the toilet bowl, I'd make patterns in them with my stream. Other times, my brother and I would stand together and have sword fights (into the bowl, not on each other). Boys pee off buildings, or outdoors, down ant holes, into camp fires, or while swimming, and it's great. Apart from taking care not to get it caught in a zipper, or having to worry about a blow to the groin—either of which only has to happen once to teach a lesson no male forgets—the penis is essentially a worry-free, low-maintenance appendage.

But all the while a boy is growing up, he's gathering information about sex, even before he learns that his penis is going to have something to do with it. He watches how his parents touch each other, or he observes people on TV giggling about sex, rolling their eyes, or licking their chops, and he files it all away, without knowing what it means. Girls certainly become more interesting, but the mechanics of sex remain unclear.

Maybe a year or so before puberty, a young boy starts hearing stories from older boys about "wet dreams." Curiosity is piqued. "Like when you dream you're swimming?" the young boy asks. The older boy says no. "You mean you dream you wet the bed?" "No, stupid," he says scornfully, "you know—nocturnal emissions." I didn't like the sound of that at all. Whatever they were, I was pretty sure I didn't want nocturnal emissions sneaking up on me while I was sleeping. When it finally happened, I was surprised at the strangely pleasurable sensation, but also frightened, and embarrassed. I'd change pajamas and hide the "soiled" ones under the bed, feeling ashamed, unsure of what was happening to me.

Then "boners" start happening in broad daylight, big lumps that show right through your pants. Some girls think we do it on purpose, a little joke to play on girls while slow-dancing, but it's not true. Once I got one in biology class while watching a movie about cell division. There's nothing overtly erotic about cell division. I prayed it would go away before a girl noticed and started passing notes about it. Erections happen over and over, day or night—while you're watching TV, riding a bus on a potholed road, climbing a tree, or just sitting at the dinner table, thinking of nothing in particular. To hell with nocturnal emissions—I wasn't even sure I could avoid *diurnal* emissions, which would be an embarrassment of the highest order. There are places no boy wants to get a hard-on, like in the locker room or in church, but there just doesn't seem to be any way to avoid them.

What the boy needs, at this point, is a good sex-education class to help clear up these mysteries. My own junior high school health instructor, Mr. Donaldson, had two things to say about the penis: don't let it get syphilis, or it will fall off; and don't get girls pregnant with it, or you won't be able to go to college. No methods for avoiding conception were addressed, other than abstinence. Mr. Donaldson was good at teaching us the parts of the reproductive system, like the fallopian tubes, which for a long time I thought were Filipino tubes, or the *vas deferens*, as in "there's a vas deferens between men and women." We also learned certain statistics, such as the numbers of sperm men have and the numbers of eggs women have and how the numbers change as we grow old until they're down to zero, and then we die. Unfortunately, these classes didn't venture very far beyond anatomy and its consequences. We heard nary a word about intimacy, emotions, love, passion, or dysfunction. Whether the school board had ruled that such things had nothing to do with sex, or whether Mr. Donaldson was just too embarrassed to mention them, I'll never know. If the schools were to apply the same reticence to teaching driver's ed, half the telephone poles in this country would have Camaros wrapped around them. We now lead the developed world in teenage pregnancies and abortions, at

96 and 60 per 1,000 females respectively, against, for example, 14 and 7 per 1,000 in Holland, where contraceptives are cheap and easy to get, just as handguns are here. Maybe something good can be said to come from the AIDS epidemic if it lays to rest the "ignorance is bliss" theory and forces us to teach sex education the way it should be taught, or at least emboldens teenagers enough to get them to ask questions. In my day, even if we'd known what to ask, we'd have been too bashful to speak up.

In any case, in sex as in anything else, there's no substitute for experience. You don't learn from talking with the guys. You learn from hands-on training with girls. Even so, experience is a good but imperfect teacher. If it were perfect, it would disabuse us of the myths and misinformation we pick up from movies, dirty jokes, pornography, and sexual folklore. A sex therapist once told me he'd treated a conservative, highly religious couple who had been married for years but couldn't have children, and when he asked them what happened during intercourse, they said, "Intercourse?" They thought if you just slept side by side, you'd get kids. The misinformation people have concerning sex is stunning. While there are few grown-up "experienced" people who believe that if a woman jumps up and down after sex she won't get pregnant, or that if a man gets an erection and doesn't put it to use, he'll get sick, there are many men and women who buy a notion almost as ridiculous— that there's a standard for what "real" men "should" be, sexually.

The real man is hung like a basset hound, is able to chisel marble or knock down old hotels with his erections, gets them whenever he wants them, dozens a night unless he wants one to last till dawn, and he comes like a freight train. His women, young virgin-whores too plentiful to keep track of, have so many orgasms in a row they pass out and wake up changed. All this because a "real" man is born knowing how to make love, a natural genius on the order of Mozart. He never has doubt and never feels the need to talk about sex.

Take one aspect of this "real" man stereotype—that bigger is better. A lot of men worry that everyone else's penis is bigger than theirs and that all women prefer large penises. The truth is, few penises are inadequate for lovemaking. For one thing, a woman is much more sensitive around her vaginal opening than she is deep in her vagina. In fact, as the upper portion of the vagina "balloons" as a woman becomes excited, the length of the penis becomes even less relevant. And of course, the source of a woman's sexual pleasure is still primarily her clitoris, not her vagina. So while there are some women who are preoccupied with size, surveys indicate that most care more for the quality of the painting than the gauge of the paintbrush.

As if size isn't enough for the "real" man to worry about, he's also supposed to be perfectly potent. In fact, a male's sexual responses are no more predictable than a female's.

Let's go back to Dick and Jane for a moment. There are any number of reasons for Dick to have failed to get an erection, anything from having had too much to drink to feeling overworked at the office to remembering a magazine article about impotence that scared him. Maybe something threw him off—the phone rang, the cat meowed to be let out, or Jane jumped out of bed to put *Bolero* on the stereo. Maybe he wasn't really in the mood to make love but thought he should try because "real" men are supposed to be like batteries, ever ready and charged all the time.

Whatever the reason for Dick's initial difficulty in getting aroused, once he suspected he might not get an erection, he began looking for signs of impending doom, checking in on himself like an independent (and worried) observer, watching from across the room. Sexual self-consciousness is the end, or at least the deferment, of paradise. The more he tried not to think about getting an erection, the more he thought about it, the more there was to think about, the more he tried not to. The arousal messages to and from his penis got intercepted and usurped by the nervous static of anxiety, with poor Dick turning the volume up by trying to turn it down.

As Dick and Jane lie there in an awkward silence, listening to the wailing of far-off police sirens, they should realize that there's nothing wrong with either of them. Dick should know that pretty much all men fail, at least once. According to statistics, sexual difficulty is the number one reason men in their twenties (supposedly our sexual "prime") seek counseling or therapy. Sex is a natural function, but unlike cavemen or cows, only modern man will try to make love under unnatural—that is, stressful—circumstances. The thing for Dick and Jane to do is talk about the circumstances and what their expectations and anxieties are, and then the conditions they both need, or prefer, in order to bring out the nightingales and violins.

The taboo, though, says we can't talk about sex, admit ignorance, or confess to doubt or we will "ruin" sex. Rehashing disappointment is not my favorite pastime either, but if you don't admit ignorance, you spread it; and if you don't face doubt, you feed it. If Jane leaves a blank, Dick will fill it in for her. He'll suppose she is disappointed in his penis or else thinks it's inadequate, her silence just another way of saying *"où est le boeuf?"* There won't be any better occasion to talk about it, and the longer she waits, the less likely he'll be to mention it, unless it happens again, and that's only if he's willing to risk failure twice. He might figure he'll feel more at ease with Jane a second time and thus see her again. But he might recall his chagrin, add up the pluses and the minuses, and in all that math forget her phone number.

Far and away the best reason to discuss a case of impotence is that the odds are, sex is not the problem. Dysfunction is often the first indicator that something else is troubling a man. In that sense, the penis is like a canary in the coal mine of the psyche. We—men and women both—think of the penis as an isolated *part* so much that we forget about the whole. Men, like women, are whole bodies, governed by a complex mixture of emotions, upbringing, and tradition. Men are not just penises, any more than sex is just hydraulics.

Having said that, it would be wrong to deny the extent to which men really do identify with their penises because of the tremendous amount of pleasure they get from them. Part of the reason men buy into the hyperbole of the "real" man is that it offers them a concrete definition of masculinity to refer to when the mysteries of love and sex overwhelm them. And in the final analysis, a degree of exultation does justice to the grandiosity we feel when everything goes right, when an organ which 99 percent of the time is just housing for a urinary conduit suddenly insists upon itself in a robustly emotional way. It would be a mistake to think the penis is only a source of worry, because it is also a source of great joy, equally a writer's obligation to describe. But how?

A man naked and erect with a woman, open to her scrutiny and appraisal, is never as vulnerable, but at the same time probably never as vain, feeling like a peacock in full display. He'll take the smallest compliment profoundly to heart, believe it immediately, and remember it a long time. Sometimes the look on a woman's face is compliment enough.

An erect penis shines and swells with life, but most of all it feels beautiful. I can't say for certain what other men experience, but when my penis is inside a woman, it feels that it's exactly where it belongs, doing exactly what it's supposed to do. The closer I get to orgasm, the more encompassing the sensations become, until finally, it's as if I'm infusing my lover with every part of my body, every tensed muscle, every rushing cell. Our hearts beat in synchrony, I'm certain of it. We are as physically close to each other as we'll ever get, and, for a while, I don't know my name, I can't count to three, and the difference between night and day is beyond me. For some indefinable period of time, there is no longer any separation between mind and body. Gradually, the eternal schism re-establishes itself, and paradise is lost once more, but the memory lingers, of a transcendent wholeness. Sometimes afterward, I feel like laughing at how ineffably swell everything is.

I think it can take men, maybe the majority of us, quite some time to learn to live with ourselves and accept our sexuality, learn to know what to expect, what the myths are and what the reality is. It's even more difficult because it's not a simple trial-and-error learning process—there's someone else there with him, trying and erring right along with him, to feel ashamed or humiliated in front of. Fortunately, exploring the mystery together has its rewards as well.

Sisters

■

"I'm rubber and you're glue," she says. "Everything bounces off me and sticks to you." She ducks behind the couch, just in time to dodge the pillow he has thrown at her.

"Oh yeah?" he says.

"Yeah," she says, sticking her head up. He nails her square in the forehead with a blast from his squirt gun.

"No fair," she says. "Just for that, I'm going to cover you with girl germs," leaping over the back of the couch to attack.

"You and whose army?" he says. He empties his water pistol at her, but on she comes. She digs her fingers deep into his ribs and tickles him until he drops his gun. He rolls over and tickles her, sitting on her stomach, pinning her arms to the floor.

"You're hurting me," she says, freeing one hand.

"No, I'm not," he says.

"Yes, you are—ouch," she says. She slugs him in the arm. "I mean it."

"Geez," he says, getting off her. "Be touchy, why don't you?"

"Why can't you admit it when you're wrong, instead of being a jerk about it?" she says. "You never do." It has gotten a little serious.

"I'm not a jerk," he says. "I'm wrong, okay? I'm sorry if I hurt you."

"Well, okay," she says. "I'll let it go. This time."
They kiss.

Up to the kiss, this could have been a brother and sister, each about ten years old. In fact, it's a fictitious (and cleaned-up) but representative scenario of how my girlfriend and I would horse around sometimes. We'd joke, give each other grief, make fun of each other's habits, bust each other up and make faces, and have tempers that flash and flare from time to time. All the while, one thing was clear to us—if other parts of our relationship were ambiguous or unresolved, be that as it may, we definitely got along well. This was important to us, a fact we could depend on in times of doubt. We had an easy way of playing together, we had fun, and when we fought, we resolved our disputes quickly, as if there were some invisible parental presence standing over us saying, "Now you two—knock it off!" The reason, I'm sure, had something to do with the fact that in certain ways, I was like the brother she grew up with, and she was like my sisters.

If there is a war going on between the sexes, then a sibling rivalry between a brother and a sister is the boot camp, the place where we hold war games and train, learning both to compete and cooperate with each other. When I grew up, the sides were even, my brother, Dan, two years younger than me, and I against our sisters—Bekka, two years older than me, and Suzu, four years younger. We taught each other how to be friends. Sexual compatibility is one thing, but it probably wouldn't mean much unless you are socially compatible as well, and we first learn to socialize in our families.

Maybe in super-wealthy TV families like the Carringtons or the Ewings it's different, but fortunately, we were just an ordinary American midwestern family, unsaddled with the burden of oil billions to fight over, so we always got along well. We get together now for holidays or special occasions, and I love seeing my sisters. Sometimes I'm away so long that I'm afraid they won't recognize me, but they always do, usually greeting me with a hug and a hearty, "Wow—*you've* gained weight." I smile and chuckle at their *greatly exaggerated* joke. They are cool women.

I can think of four kinds of sisters. Rarest would be a twin, which I thankfully never had. An absolute equal of the opposite sex would have been too confusing. Plus we always got to design our own birthday menus, something I would not have enjoyed sharing. Next would be half-sisters from previous marriages, or in Cinderella's case, evil stepsisters. I had no evil steps either. I did have one each of the two most common kinds, older and younger. Fascinating studies have been done on how kids develop according to their position in the family, but I've never seen the results subdivided according to gender, have never read if oldest boys are different from oldest girls—all I know, personally, is that an older sister is different from a younger one, and that both had different effects on me.

My older sister Rebecca goes by the name Bekka, spelled that way since before I can remember why, except she never liked "Becky" or the Sunnybrook Farm jokes that went with "Rebecca." She liked me because I was the first doll she ever had. This partly describes the problem with older sisters—mainly, that they think they're in charge of you from the minute you're born, and they occasionally treat younger brothers the way younger brothers occasionally treat family cats, with what might be called "ruthless affection." I don't think it's entirely due to a defense of territory, siblings rivaling each other for parental attention, competing for nest space. Older sisters are already part of the familial establishment, and don't really know they're just kids too—they think of themselves as parents. Real parents often reinforce this illusion by saying things like "Bekka, why don't you and your brother pick up your toys?" as my father would say, before I was old enough to understand complicated instructions, or "Bekka, will you please keep an eye on Peter while I lie around watching soap operas while the entire house goes to seed?" as my mother was always saying. It wasn't the things Bekka made me do that I remember, as much as how she threatened me if I didn't do them. One of my earliest memories is of when I was about three. She'd learned a new word from Judy Reese across the street, and for a while, if I didn't do something she wanted me to do, such as wash my hands for dinner, Bekka would say she was going to "*sue* me for all I was worth." I asked what *sue* meant, and she said it's where you go to court and the judge gives you everything the other person has. I didn't have much—a pair of real leather chaps, a cap gun with holster, and one of those inflatable clown-shaped punching bags with the sand in the bottom and the nose that squeaked—but still, I was terrified. I didn't want to be *sued*. I was only three. Where was I going to get a lawyer? This was perhaps why, come to think of it, my younger brother became one.

My mother's authority was beyond doubt—I could defy it, but I couldn't deny it. I gradually realized my older sister's authority was negotiable. I never actually achieved ascendancy, but I figured out how to wheel and deal, trade favors or swap duties, how to assert myself, and how to back down when it was obvious I couldn't duck out of mowing the lawn without Bekka telling Mom. Maybe parents set the moral codes in a family, but older sisters enforce them.

Boys go through a stage, from about kindergarten to fifth grade, where they are supposed to hate girls, which serves the biological function of preventing us from getting married until we have enough money to move out. Officially, girls were slow and weak, cried easily, and gave long-winded overwritten book reports. This is the period when actual fistfights between the sexes break out on playgrounds. There was a grade school in Rhode Island where they had to supervise recess because roving gangs of girls were beating up boys. Sisters were live-in proof that if girls were the enemy, for whatever abstruse behavioral reasons, they were still all right to goof around with, so long as your male friends didn't see you. We'd fight tooth and nail, of course, over whose turn it was to do the dishes, whether cleaning the bathroom (their job) was as hard as mowing the lawn (our job) or which TV show to watch, "The Man from U.N.C.L.E." or "The Red Skelton Show," but we would also make tents under the dining room table or play Monopoly.

Affection was okay, in the privacy of our own home or during family vacations. I remember Bekka and me pretending that a hammock at the family lake cottage was a motorboat, or the time we stood at the end of a dock in green raincoats, pretending we were symphony conductors, directing a summer thunderstorm with reeds of snakegrass for batons. In public, we went separate ways. She went off with her girlfriends, while my buddies and I practiced being jerks, fighting and arguing over the rules of baseball and throwing dead fish at each other. Had we been deer, we'd have been butting each other with our tiny antlers and practicing to be adults.

Older sisters also lead younger brothers into adulthood, by word and by example. Years after you've stopped taking baths together, the day you realize your sister is becoming a woman, you learn why. This would be the day Bekka came home from a trip downtown, shopping with Jeannie Petersen, to announce that she'd bought a really cool record called "The Surfin' Bird," by the Trashmen. Jeannie bought something called "I Wanna Hold Your Hand," by someone named the Beatles. "Hold hands?" I said. "Oh gross— *mushy stuff*" (we really used that phrase), and feigned throwing up, which was usually our response to mushy stuff, but this time Bekka didn't join in. Little did I realize how much a part of my life mushy stuff would become. If she could consider it and not make a face, then I supposed I would have to consider it too.

Bekka would have dancing parties in the living room with her friends, and I'd watch. Especially Leslie Anderson. Boy, did I watch Leslie Anderson, while the Beatles music helped clarify the things I was beginning to feel. Bekka taught me to dance, how to sort of dip at the knees in time to the music, turn from side to side, and pretend I was throwing corn to chickens with both hands. She started using makeup, wearing nylons and jewelry, and going to school social events, stepping out of the androgynous uniformity of youth. Maybe it was threatening. When she began to mature physically, we teased her as much as we possibly could, calling her "Bekka the Bod" and saying she was in love with a guy we made up, named "Bill Moosey." "Where were you tonight?" I'd say. "I'll bet you snuck out with Bill Moosey," teasing her to see her reaction.

I was next in line for puberty, without a clue as to how I was going to handle it.

Our closest moment, in our early adolescence, came during another family vacation, a camping trip out west, the summer before I was supposed to enter junior high school. We were in the Grand Tetons. The rest of the family was sitting around the camp fire one night, when Bekka took me aside, saying she had something important to tell me. She was worried about me. We were sitting on the picnic table, out of earshot of our parents. We spoke in conspiratorial tones.

"Peter," she said, "you know, don't you, that in seventh grade, you're going to have to kiss girls?"

"What?" I said. I'd suspected some of my friends had begun doing this as early as sixth grade, but no one actually told me they were. "Why?"

"You just have to," she said. "Everybody does it, if you want to be cool." I definitely wanted to be cool. Then she gave me some of the best advice I ever got from anybody. "You should know though," she said, "that you can be cool and still get good grades." The future was suddenly in focus. Before then, it seemed as if you had to choose either to dissipate and rebel and be cool, or obey and study and be smart but unpopular. Cool and smart seemed antithetical, until then.

"Thanks," I said.

"It's okay," she said, hugging me.

"Can I ask you something, though?" I said.

"Anything," she said.

"Have you ever kissed Bill Moosey?"

Within a year, we were at odds again, mainly because the ways I endeavored to be cool reawoke the surrogate parent in her. Just when I thought she was going to be my ally, she started taking my parents' sides against me, whenever they caught me smoking or drinking or blowing my lunch money on bookies, fast women, and ice cream sandwiches. I couldn't believe it. Parents were that way, just because they were, but I saw no reason why one of my own had to come on like Little-Miss-High-and-Mighty-Holier-Than-Thou.

Though she was in fact holier than me. Whatever an oldest child does sets the standard (and I'll bet most of them are conscious of it) by which the other kids will be judged—they are, after all, the ones parents use as examples when they say, "Why can't you be like ———— ?" I think as a typical teenager I was rebelling against world and parents by rebelling against Bekka too, positioned halfway between me and them. Especially since it was a lot easier to yell back at her than at world or parents.

Maybe it's even logical, then, that my first significant rapprochement with Authority came when I made up with her. I learned, when I got to college, where she was a sophomore and I was a freshman, that she wasn't as holy as I'd thought, and never had been. She tried to hide it from me, and succeeded for maybe the first month, but eventually I found her out: she was smoking and drinking too! Not with my level of expertise, but still. . . . Instead of resenting the hypocrisy, something that barely occurred to me, I felt relieved. She was okay after all. She told me over a beer, in her smoke-filled dorm room, that all along, all she'd ever wanted was that I not screw up too bad; she'd been concerned that I turn out okay, and I could see it was obviously true. That reconciliation was the start of a beautiful friendship. In some sense, my first major campaign in the ongoing war between the sexes was over, an honorable and lasting peace made.

No doubt the consensus among psychiatrists would be that the most influential woman on a man's development is his mother, which I wouldn't argue with, but a female sibling would have to rank close behind. She is the equal, from whom a boy learns the politics of platonic love. Knowing the ropes of platonic love, or how to get along in a confined space with a member of the opposite gender, is probably as important to the ultimate success of a man's adult relationship with a woman as knowing the ways of romantic love, since once the initial superhots go away, we love both platonically and romantically. Platonic love is almost a kind of survival love, because it's love without a choice—you can't divorce a sister—so you learn to enjoy it. I don't know if men who grew up with sisters have better luck with relationships, fewer divorces, and better communication, than men who didn't. For me, it cuts down on surprises and makes me feel more at home.

All told, I suppose I am more comfortable in a relationship, playing the older brother, the big shot, the protector. Given a choice, I'd suppose most people would rather lead than be led. Given the way men tend to prefer younger women, this could be universally true. Playing the older brother makes me feel important, benevolent, and magnanimous when I do something nice. Being an older brother, as a kid, is a position of great power, since boys take advantage of younger sisters, right up to the moment they get old enough to realize their role in life is not to turn the television channel or get sandwiches for their older brothers. The disproportion in power and authority is there to exploit. Then too, the baby in any family tends to get the most affection and/or attention, and often returns it, doting unconditionally on his or her older siblings, certainly more than they at least dote on each other.

My younger sister's given name is Suzanne, but we've called her Suzu ever since my brother, Dan, mispronounced her name on the way home from the hospital, the day she was born. From that moment on, she was *ours*. Some boys treat younger sisters worse than they treat cats. Dan and I were a little better. At least we waited until she was old enough to put up a little resistance before we started torturing her. The first forms we devised for her were purely physical, our preferred method, an exercise in punishment we called the "up-downs," in which we threw her to the floor, and then one of us held her hands while the other sat on her stomach and bounced up and down. This was particularly effective because it prevented her from screaming for help, her cries coming out, "Ma-ah-ah-ah-ah-ah-ah-ah-mmm-uh!" Eventually though, her cries were heard, and we had to switch from physical to psychological torture. The high moment of my brother's and my career assailing Suzu's mental health probably came, not by coincidence, on her favorite day of the year, Christmas Eve, when she was about eight or nine. It was her job to distribute the Christmas presents— no one was allowed to begin opening them until they were all out from under the tree. This Christmas, her eyes grew wider and wider with excitement, as she realized that her pile of loot, for some reason, was easily twice the size of anybody else's. "Wow," she said, "I've got *lots* more presents than you do," and it was true, because Danny and I had given them to her. What we'd done, basically, was go into her room and wrap up a whole bunch of items she already had, her old dolls, her shoes, her clothes, and so on. Needless to say, she was crushed with disappointment after the third or fourth familiar thing she unwrapped, and ran upstairs in tears. It seemed like a good idea at the time.

I don't know why boys do this, opting for violence or mistreatment, but to be fair, they do it to everything, animate and inanimate, toys, baby sisters, pets, each other, garbage-can lids, trees. It's androgen poisoning. The forms of interpersonal aggression mature as we mature, but there is always competition—physical, then psychological, in ever-refining degrees of subtlety. In the struggle for both parental love and self-esteem, we seem to have chosen, in our family, divergent rather than convergent paths, not a whole family of tennis players, but one where everyone chose something different. Between ourselves, we worked it out in mock battles, learning the limits, what we could do and what we couldn't. We learn early when we've gone too far in our exuberance and actually hurt someone. It's a process of trial and error.

Suzu grew up with a great sense of humor anyway. She was always putting on shows for the family, doing magic tricks in which things disappeared when she put them behind her back, or shows where we used to take all the clothes off Barbie and Ken and then . . . uh . . . well, that was more just for the kids than for the family. She made all the boyfriends Bekka ever brought home play the home version of "Jeopardy" with her, which might be why Bekka had so few dates in high school. Suzu wrote a textbook on how to be cute that is still being widely used by girls across America. She would do characters and voices—Lily Tomlin is about the only person I can think of comparing her to. Doubtless it's her style, her big personality, and her appreciation for the silly and the absurd that's helped determine the kind of sense of humor I suppose I look for in a woman. A girlfriend even commented once that she felt she was competing with Suzu.

"What?" I said. "That's crazy."

"You always talk about her," I was told.

Maybe to an extent it was true. I, of course, had a lot of family stories to use as examples of what I knew or expected from someone I lived with. I'm sure I used Suzu more than once, perhaps to excess, as an example of the kind of attitude I admired and/or missed. Maybe I used her as an example because our relationship has a sort of lasting innocence, a friendship without the conundrum of sex thrown in to befuddle and obscure everything, that no girlfriend could hope (or want) to match. Someone once said that to be happy, you should go to a small town, find the youngest daughter in a large family, and marry her. Anyone who had a lot of older siblings would grow up a tolerant person. What I want as much as anything from a woman is the same kind of respect and loyalty Suzu has for me. We still disagree and criticize, but it doesn't diminish the fondness we feel for each other. Women who have older brothers, in spite or because of being teased, tested, and tortured by them, seem to be a lot more understanding and therefore forgiving of my boyish ways, my need to belch and be loud now and then. They're not shocked, or judgmental. I'm more appreciative of someone's girlish ways for the same reason.

Watching an older sister become an adult woman is new and fascinating, but seeing the same process transform a baby sister is both wonderful and a little sad, because as a big brother, you almost don't want it to happen, especially when your friends start telling you what a hot number your baby sister is becoming. It cultivates a desire to protect and care for women, not in any chauvinist sense, but purely because you start to have an idea of the kind of evil that's out there. Maybe it's the guilt for causing her so much grief catching up with you, but the result is a noble sentiment. Suzu was in high school when I was in college, but I would come home for holidays and try to catch up on how she was changing, who she was seeing. When I had graduated and she was in college, I would occasionally drive down to visit her, teach her how to drink beer, meet her friends. We probably grew closer than we'd ever been at home. A friend of mine said his little sister called him the night she lost her virginity. "Maybe that seems a little strange, but you can just *talk* to little sisters," he told me. "I don't know why." I thought of the time I called Suzu, after a woman I was living with had told me she was leaving, and I was devastated and heartbroken, with no idea where to turn. I think we talked for two or three hours that night. She didn't have vast resources of romantic experience to call upon and advise me from, but she had all the sympathy I could have ever hoped for, and the kind of steadfast loyalty I needed to be reminded still existed.

Growing older, of course, also means growing apart. Shortly after that, I went home for Christmas. We had the usual family celebration, minus Bekka, who by then had married and moved away to Montana. Suzu distributed the presents, and we made jokes about the time we gave her the stuff she already had. We called Bekka long distance and eventually went to bed. Another family tradition was to wake up real early Christmas Day, and run downstairs in our pajamas and open our stockings, which Santa had filled overnight with a tangerine, a brazil nut, and a shiny penny. We didn't have a fireplace, so we tied our stockings to an antique pump organ. If you stood back and squinted, it sort of looked like a fireplace. Suzu insisted that we all continue to wake up early and run down the stairs in our pajamas. I'd grumbled every year that I was getting too old for it and I wanted to sleep and just be left alone, but I always threw on a robe and went along with it. This Christmas I grumbled again, and this time they let me sleep. "You'll be sorry," Suzu said. I woke up about eleven, and everyone else's presents were opened, stockings emptied, and everyone was out cross-country skiing or running around. I started picking at what "Santa" brought me, all by myself, and felt about as rotten and lonely and empty as I've ever felt. I said as much to Suzu later, and she said something to the effect of "I told you so." In some sense, she knew how I'd felt because, in a way, a sister is as close as a man will ever come to having his own feminine half come to life, a sort of model for what he'd be if he'd been born female and raised under all the same influences. Who knows? You should listen to the people who know you best when they say, "You'll be sorry."

A man learns from loving and living with sisters the need to preserve the traditions and structures of love. You just do things together, and if you do them long enough, they become the way you love each other, washing the dishes, eating meals. You love a sister not uncritically but unquestionably. As Robert Frost said, "Home is the place where, when you have to go there, they have to take you in." You have no high hopes that the love of a sister will get better; nor do you fear it will get suddenly worse and die, as might romantic love. You learn to love not under pressure. You learn what you can get away with and what you can't, how far to push, when not to, how to share, how to listen, how to argue, how to leave someone alone, how to simply be polite, and how to value someone for who they are, as the cliché goes, because you've known them all your life. You've both bailed out of the same nest. In the long run, old conflicts become water over the dam, because you realize how much you need each other. You are each other's oldest friends.

Bekka today is living with her husband in Great Falls, Montana. She has two boys, who love "Masters of the Universe" dolls more than life itself, having pitched battles between them constantly, making up for their lack of sisters to do battle with. Bekka was the first to go off and marry and have kids, and she still leads me by the example of her maturity and good sense, her cheer and her centeredness. I think often of how much fun she must have in that house with those boys. She was always the smartest, spends what spare time she has now devouring books, always got good grades, and as far as I can tell, in the school of life, is still getting them.

Suzu is the Mary Tyler Moore of the eighties, a news producer for a Minneapolis television station. In fact, a magazine writer from New York once interviewed her on the phone and asked her if she did the same sorts of things Mary Richards did at her job on the show.

"What did Mary Richards ever do?" Suzu said. Suzu does much more.

She has friends over often. She marks the height of all of them on her kitchen door with a pencil. She goes fishing and camping. On Friday nights, she and her pals sing at a piano bar. She's married to Kirk, one heckuva lovable galoot, she'd be the first to admit. They have a nice house. We still talk on the phone for hours, when we're in trouble and when we're not. She reminds me of important birthdays and anniversaries. She keeps me posted, and she won't let me get away with anything. I need my sisters. If they were ever to drop out of touch with me, I'd . . . why I'd . . . I'd *sue* them for everything they're worth. Yeah, that's what I'd do. Even if they did both marry lawyers. I'll hire my brother.

Getting Involved Anyway

■

Fear of Commitment

■

If you want to scare your boyfriend next Halloween, come dressed as what he fears most. Commitment. It shouldn't cost much to put the costume together, a wedding veil, a set of bloodsucking fangs, a pillow to simulate pregnancy under a kitchen apron, and a set of claws or hooks for your hands. You'll be the horrible embodiment of an average male's favorite pet bogeyman, or in this case, bogey-woman: Love the Destroyer, Leveler of Bachelorly Worlds. It speaks well for love that for all the fear of commitment going around, men and women still commit themselves to each other on a regular basis, succumbing to the mystical power of it. But not, as is the case when human beings have to deal with most mystical powers, without a struggle. It happened to me one summer, not too long ago. There I was, hanging out, minding my own business, not looking for trouble, feeling fine. In April, my girlfriend Alice and I had broken up, concluding with mutual sadness and regret that whatever it was we'd had for three years had flown, the decision to "just be friends" more or less a decision to keep things the way they'd been for a long time anyway. I wasn't crushed. I was footloose and fancy free, single, healthy, and it was summer. I almost had a tan. My plan was to kick back, lay low, underachieve, have fun, and *just date*. Just date.

Nothing heavy.

In August I headed up to Vermont, to attend a writers' conference. These are events where writers confer, share their work, drink copious amounts of alcohol, and have brief affairs. So I'd heard. It was going to be a vacation. I'd play it by ear, meet other writers, people with interests and occupations similar to mine, and kiss the ones that were female, if they wanted to, and if not, fine.

Nothing heavy.

There was a large rustic building at this conference, kind of a lounge/snack shop, called the Barn, and in the Barn, there was a grand piano. So I was minding my own business, not looking for trouble, when I heard someone playing Rodgers and Hart tunes on the piano. This was when a funny thing happened.

A woman sang. I heard her voice.

Remember the part in *The Odyssey*, where they sail past the Sirens, who sing so beautifully that whoever hears them falls instantly in love with them, so Ulysses has his men put wax in their ears and then lash him to the mast so he can hear them sing? I didn't have any wax in my ears, or at least not enough, and no men, and no mast for them to lash me to if I'd had men. Defenseless, I ambled over to the piano to see who was singing. Call her Laurel. I introduced myself.

We circled each other warily for three days. We were playing our cards close to the vest, chatting idly, joining each other casually for meals, seeing if the interest might be mutual, and looking for the most obvious entry-level incompatibilities, ascertaining that we weren't gay, married, Republican, or incubating horrible diseases, and didn't have webbed feet. One morning I saw her again in the Barn, sipping tea from a Styrofoam cup.

"Laurel," I said. "Guess what?"

"What?" she said.

"I think I'm getting a crush on you," I said.

She blushed beet red, and her eyes lit up. It froze her in her tracks.

"You too?" I asked.

She nodded, a slight look of terror on her face. She continued on her way without saying anything. I couldn't say anything either. The butterflies in my stomach wouldn't let me. If I opened my mouth, one might have flown out and given me away. It had begun, and so had the terror of it all.

Anybody who has ever felt those butterflies would have to admit that they are not entirely tremblings of pure and pleasing wonder. When I fall in love, I start having dreams with lost-in-the-maze motifs. I'd almost suspect anyone who says they've fallen in love and not felt at least *some* degree of trepidation would be either lying or crazy. The degree varies, and fear of love covers a lot of territory, but when the degree is sufficient to deter the continuance of a relationship, we call it fear of commitment.

I'm not sure that when men and women talk about commitment, they're talking about the same thing. I saw a story on television where three mountain men—three toothless dirty sexist bearded smelly mountain men, living in shipping-crate shacks one hundred miles from civilization, panning for gold in Alaska, took an ad out in a newspaper for mail-order brides, and they got over 4,000 responses from women willing to move to the bottom of a frozen swamp and live with morons they'd never even met. I don't get it. What's the thinking here? That commitment for commitment's sake will make everything all right and transform a shack into a castle? Reverse the sexes, and I don't think there are 4,000 men who would take the same chance.

Being and living alone does not seem to hold the terror for men that it does for some women. Maybe we're both irrational, women wanting the security of commitment more than they should, men fearing it more than they ought. For my part, as far back as I can remember, before it ever had anything to do with love or women, being free was better than having obligations, free to climb trees or catch salamanders instead of having to go to some ice cream social with the family. Most of my male friends say roughly the same thing, that the first dozen happy childhood memories that come to mind involve being out of the house, horsing around, inculcating a need for freedom and independence that commitment runs contrary to. And wasn't it always a woman who was bent on curtailing my freedom, as in my mother, as in, "Peter, stop playing with those electric wires or I'll ground you"?

Not that we all have mother complexes, but it's different. Women see being a part of a committed relationship as enriching, a bonded partnership in life, an opportunity to excel, become better than you could be on your own, exercise and revel in your own ability to love. Companionship is empowerment, a celebration of all that is best about being a feeling, caring human being.

Many men see this as a trap. I'd guess most women have found themselves, at least once, on the wrong end of a man's trap-a-phobia, her affection misinterpreted, told she's being too clingy, trying to "get her hooks into him," when she sees herself as being only well intentioned. You never hear about men having "hooks." A "clingy" woman is exactly what a man is afraid of becoming, weak and needy, so he has to fight back, the same way schoolyard bullies beat up the weak kids because they fear their own weakness. I have known guys so leery of involvement that they're not even polite about saying so. Rudeness is undeniably effective at warding off unwanted love. What could be so terrifying about commitment that it can turn a seemingly nice fellow into a flaming you-know-what?

Usually nothing, but that's the point. Fears are a loss of proportion, the imagination's exaggeration. The word *irrational* suggests an unequal ratio, things out of balance. Initially, a man facing the prospect of commitment thinks more about how bad it could be than how good, and his single past suddenly looks better than he thought it was—one way or another, a *colossal* change looms imminent. Married people always say it's not really that different, but conscience makes cowards of us all who aren't. All it takes sometimes is someone singing Rodgers and Hart to knock you off stride.

Laurel lived a hundred miles from me, a do-able commute, but far enough that I could have let the whole thing slide and blamed it on the inconvenience. My pleasant, obligation-free, and productive summer started to look extraordinary, the last days of the life I knew as a free man in Paris, and I was almost missing it before it was over. When Laurel and I parted at the end of the conference, though I felt impossibly great about having met her,

I wondered if maybe I ought not to just keep going the way I was, concentrate on things other than romance for a while. I knew the statistics, that men can afford to postpone romantic involvement, work on their careers, and find fulfillment in that, until their forties, and still have reasonable expectations. There was an Ivy League study, featured in *People* magazine, that suggested that women over thirty stood a very poor chance of marrying, while men's odds don't start going down until much later, a study that was much argued with and contradicted by other studies, but all Laurel and I knew was, I wasn't in a hurry, and since she was younger than I, neither was she. I heard no biological clock. If I wanted romance, why not just play the field? I had prospects. Without being able to say where commitment might lead, I knew where it certainly would not—down any number of avenues of adventure. I couldn't move to the South of France with Brooke Shields, for example. I'm not kidding. That's what I mean by "out of proportion." I had wild fantasies like that—what if Brooke got down on her hands and knees and begged me? What would I do then? Was I ready to give up all hope?

Two things convinced me to see Laurel again. I went to my sister's wedding, where I played the bachelor brother, the last single kid in the family, and between the real or imagined pressure I felt, and the serious pleasure my sister was taking in her new committed life, I didn't utter the "M" word out loud, but I started pronouncing it silently in my head, just to see how it sounded. Maybe it was time I became a responsible adult. Or something. Maybe. More to the point, every time I thought of Laurel, I felt, literally, a sort of golden glow inside. From fear? Awe? Undeniably, when I thought of her and of what the situation was.

Something heavy.

She came down to visit three weeks after we'd last seen each other. I was up to my eyeballs in apprehension, if not panic. What if the attraction we'd felt was gone? What if we'd only been fooling ourselves? A large part of the fear of commitment, for men, is the fear we're fooling ourselves, don't really know ourselves well enough to make that kind of promise. Fear of falling in love is the fear you'll fall out of love later, when the consequences will be far worse—the blues if you're *lucky*, and the infliction of real pain and anguish if you're not, and usually you're not lucky. How *do* you know yourself well enough?

I mulled over what I know about myself. I have friends who admit to an uncontrollable sexuality and don't even try to commit, because they're "just not built that way," not a "one-woman man," Peter Pans prolonging the free ride of casual affection and easy lust for as long as possible, making "nothing heavy" their life's motto. I was raised to believe that path is ultimately less fulfilling, but I can see with my own eyes it would certainly be less difficult. And I know how lazy I can be, or want to be. You could go a long time living moment to moment, and there seem to be more independent, commitment-shy career-oriented women to circulate among than ever. Commitment holds the promise of richness, security, true companionship, but who was I kidding? I'd been through this before. It's hard work too. Nobody pretends otherwise. I hate hard work. Ask anybody.

After the second time I visited Laurel, I was sure of one thing. My worst suspicions were confirmed—she was exactly as marvelous a human being as I'd first thought. Not perfect but, in all probability, *the one for me.* The more I thought that, the more it worried me. I'd felt something was right twice before, and had committed myself, only to learn I'd been mistaken. And once I got so thoroughly rejected that I was a wreck for almost two years. How could I risk that again? And I was only half afraid she'd reject me. I was plagued with self-doubt, the fear I'd hurt her by screwing up again. She was too kind, too loving, much righter for me, being as objective as I could be, than any of the others. It would have been easier if something was wrong with her, if there were some sort of excuse for failure built into the situation, but there wasn't. Any disaster was probably going to be my fault. The gravity of the responsibility of holding another person's happiness in your hands doesn't always dawn on a man until after it's too late. I do know some things about myself: I'm not easy to live with. I have long suits, but I have short ones too, and it has to be that way. I'm Peter Nelson, not Ozzie, no steady-tempered, mild-mannered, easygoing, becardiganed doo-fus, and I don't see that changing—I wouldn't want it to. As the line in the Tom Waits song goes, "if I exorcised my devils, my angels may leave too." Would it be fair to ask Laurel to put up with me? A lot of guys can see themselves as doing the woman a favor by refusing to commit—the less involved she is, the better for her in the long run.

The third time I went to visit Laurel, I knew I was going to tell her I loved her. This was or still is as much of a statement of commitment as I am capable of making. I don't say it if I don't mean it. I knew it was true, and I knew I was going to tell her, even though I wanted to wait. It had been a mere month. I wanted to be surer. I wanted her to go first. That way, if years later everything were to deteriorate and we'd break up, I could point a finger at her and say, "Yeah, well you started it." I ran over all the counterarguments in my head, trying to live out the next few years imaginatively and flag down any problems that might arise, any last excuse to turn back.

"Hey, Laurel, guess what?"

"What?"

"I love you."

She blushed.

"You too?"

She nodded.

There are, of course, couples who talk about how much they love each other but refuse to commit. I know one couple who've lived together for almost five years now, and he still hasn't even said "I love you" to her. Maybe what you say doesn't matter all that much, as if what you speak out loud constitutes a magical incantation. In my friend's case, his fear of committing himself almost amounts to superstition. And then, there are couples who say they love each other all the time, but who run around having affairs. A friend of mine who's been married happily for years told me even though he felt he was as committed as he can be, he can't stop himself from resisting it, from wanting to run away, run amok, "especially in the fall—that was always the time of year I'd get excited about meeting new women. You have to learn to live with it." He would never run either away or amok, except in his fantasies. Even so, while he enjoys the security of commitment, it goes at least partly against his nature.

Two months into my relationship with Laurel, I found myself edging up to a new plateau. Just saying "I love you" didn't feel like enough. I was feeling so fondly toward her that I felt on the verge of suggesting a fairly common proposition to her, involving the formalization of our concomitant goals and aspirations through the performance of ritual rites and ceremonies and the exchange of symbolic jewelry otherwise known by a word beginning with "M." It was on the tip of my tongue. I never had to seriously wonder if that was what I really wanted to do, until I knew I'd met the person I'd want to do it with. I could stop myself from saying anything only by telling myself this much could wait, that it really was far too early to be throwing "M" words around. I couldn't tell what the proper timing should be—in the old days, people held hands for nine years before throwing "M" words around, but then, too, sometimes they married at thirteen—I only knew, probably from my experiences wrangling with used-car salesmen, not to jump into anything or let the hard-sell fast-paced mood of the eighties get to me.

We compromised by moving in together. It was obviously what we wanted to do, the way to make things continue to go forward, committed to getting to know each other as thoroughly as possible before making further commitments, which seemed wise and cautious. That's the problem, dealing with an f.o.c.-afflicted man. As with any fear, you can't know it won't hurt you until you let it try. Therapists who work with phobic people to desensitize them to whatever they fear—snakes, open spaces, or whatever—work in tiny increments toward confronting the snakes or the open spaces, just a little bit closer each week, slow but steady, patiently.

The traditional method for treating the f.o.c.-impaired is *playing hard to get*, and it will buy time and allow a man to continue in the familiar role of pursuer, until he's ready to commit, thinking it's his own idea and not something forced upon him. You can't *make* someone love you, but if you can't, you might be able to make yourself more lovable, not to mention secure, by learning to relax. You could talk to him about the sureness of mortality, a good antidote to the Peter Pan fantasy.

If I wasn't sure of myself, Laurel was. That made me want to take the chance. To some extent, I was no doubt committed the minute I heard her singing Rodgers and Hart at the grand piano, and the rest of it was just wondering what had happened. It was a frighteningly mysterious thing, so I wrestled with it, hated it, grew into it. When men break a relationship off, citing an unwillingness to make a commitment as the reason, they are playing it safe, rather than facing the unknown. *Courage* seems a key word here, not as a final answer but as a way of seeking it.

A Few Good Women

■

In *The Big Chill*, the young woman lawyer, played by Mary Kay Place, delivers a kitchen soliloquy which amounts to something like the modern woman's lament. It went, roughly: "They're either married or taken or gay, or recently divorced and not ready to make a commitment, or recently divorced and too ready to make a commitment, or crazy."

Picky picky picky.

Maybe it's true that good men are hard to find, but good women aren't exactly falling out of the trees everywhere you look either. They say even regular normal okay people are resorting to computer dating services, and I'm not altogether ready to doubt that, because among my circle of friends are one or two normal okay regular guys, and they wonder the same thing: Where are all the good women?

First of all, I can't tell if the good ones are really taken, or if something about being taken makes the ones I know look so good. It seems true that the best women I know are either married or might as well be. When I'm hanging out with married women, the unstated but given reality that the game is definitely *not* afoot seems to make them more relaxed, honest, and genuine around me, easier to talk to and a lot of fun. Sometimes they even try to date vicariously by setting you up with their single friends, friends who will no doubt tell them all about it the next day, but even so, it's the sort of selfless concern any man would respond to. Afterward you go home and beat either your dog or your head against the wall a few hundred times in frustration, until the neighbors complain about the noise and you have to stop.

The problem is that waiting to chance into someone who is not only terrific but also completely unencumbered is like waiting for Halley's Comet—once every seventy-six years, it will pay off. I meet plenty of women who seem to occupy a kind of middle zone between being totally dedicated to a relationship and being free. I shy away from people in semidedicated relationships. You don't want to pay other people's relationships less respect than you'd ask them to pay yours. And if I stole someone else's girlfriend, I'd either lose the right to despise the guys who steal mine or have to live with an unhealthy level of hypocrisy. Or both.

There's nowhere else to turn, then, but to the pool of women who may be slightly encumbered, dating someone without being involved, but who are otherwise legitimately "available." Of course, any time anybody, male or female, meets someone who is unattached, the first response is "Why—are you strange?" When I get past that, I find too often I meet women who fall into one of three categories.

The first group is people who haven't had enough yet. Probably though not necessarily young, these are ambitious women who still believe the world is replete with boundless promise, women who treat the possibility of a relationship like a job offer in Houston, something you try for a time while you look for something better. I have no problem with people in an all-out pursuit of personal fulfillment, but I still cherish the idea that some day someone might be as interested in my happiness as in her own.

The second group is people who've begun to suspect they've had enough. These are women who are much more earnest, cautious, who have been around the block and know too much—they are seriously looking for something meaningful and lasting, but they refuse to lower their expectations, and they overexamine everything. They want someone perfect. Superman. We've gotten the notion that life is perfectible from watching television commercials, where in the first ten seconds they tell you why you're not happy, in the middle ten seconds they show you the object you need to buy to be happy, and then in the last ten seconds they show happy people holding the object. The object women in the second group want is the one promised them in fiction and/or fantasy, a rich handsome brilliant kind stable doctor/lawyer. No man could live up to the standards these women set. I'm not inclined to try to do so.

You graduate from that state of perfectionist wantfulness to a third class of people who have definitely had enough of unfulfillment, heartache, and loneliness, until a sort of maintenance-level despair sets in. I can be just as leery of women who are not critical enough as of those who are too critical, especially women who look at me not with bedroom eyes but with delivery-room eyes. It's an odd combination, expectations simultaneously too high and too low, but it makes me doubt I could meet either halfway.

It shouldn't be so difficult. There are good women out there, and good men too, and yet sometimes it feels as if we're hiding from each other when in fact we're looking as hard as we can for each other. I can't explain it. I re-examine my own criteria. I want: someone who's already happy; who will be with me because she *wants* to be, not because she needs to be; someone I can't fool, but who enjoys it when I try; who has brains to spare and a heart the size of Greenland; who has enough self-confidence to be able to laugh at herself, and not take it all so seriously; who takes life seriously; who won't lead more than she follows or follow more than she leads; who likes dogs, beer, baseball, sex, working on old cars, or whatever, as well as likes things I don't and can teach me why I should and how I can too; who likes me, more than a little. I don't see how that's asking too much.

At least it's true that the more I look, the more I know what to look for. If I remind myself not to be too critical or too cynical, give up too soon or overexamine everything, then maybe I won't look beyond the good women I do meet. They say when you're in love, it feels like everything you've ever wanted anyway. They said Halley's Comet was coming too, and it did, didn't it? Of course, only once every seventy-six years.

My Dream Date

■

Suppose Halley's Comet comes and I meet someone. Obviously we have to date. What is the perfect date?

Two people in candlelight, a man in a tux, a woman in an evening gown, sit across from each other at a table, nibbling veal medallions between probing soul treks into each other's eyes, in a restaurant so swank the busboys speak five languages. He's got two tickets in his pocket to see Liza Minnelli in Robert Wilson's musical production of *Hedda Gabler*, and she's got a bottle of Korbel's on ice at her place for later. A waiter sets a bouquet of roses on the table, followed by the rose steward, who sniffs them and pronounces them, "Exquisite, boldly floral yet not pushily *sachet.*"

"I hope you don't mind, Amanda," the man says. "I had them flown in from Martinique. I find the volcanic soil there gives them a certain smoky *savoir-faire.*" She blushes.

"Oh Jacques," she says demurely. "Take off your eye patch—I want to see you."

That is not my idea of a dream date, two people playing dress-up and trying to impress each other, following courtship rituals just to get into each other's . . . uh . . . diaries. For me, the more I'm *supposed* to have a good time, or the greater my expectations are, the worse it usually goes. I hate trying to plan out a good time, and I always have. Between the ages of thirteen and eighteen, I lost approximately a year of that time staring at the telephone, trying to think of what I was going to say to whoever I was afraid

81

to call, and what we were going to do. I'd finally screw my courage up enough to dial and then mumble, "Uh, hi, uh, like, I was wondering, you know, if, uh, maybe, I don't know, you'd like to go to a movie or something?"

"That depends," she'd say. "Who is this?"

Traditionally, it has fallen to the man to orchestrate the big night out, which is a kind of pressure to perform, albeit an administrative one. I don't welcome it. I just want to spend time with someone, not put on "The Pete Nelson Show" for her.

Whether we are just getting to know each other, or if I'm heading out with someone I've known a long time, the key to a fun date is the spirit in which it is undertaken, that of casual adventure. It can involve going somewhere I've never gone, or doing something I've never done. If we end up milking a cow, or baking bread, I'll remember that longer than if we've only gone to another bar for another drink. Corny or strange beats boring or forced.

On my dream date, I pick my bachelorette up at seven. She's not exactly dressed up, but she has managed to put together an outfit that makes the evening seem special. She's wearing white knee socks.

It's my dream. I can have her wear what I want.

We begin by each proposing three things to do. I refuse to be completely in charge. My position is, If you want to be led somewhere, date a seeing-eye dog. She says she wants to eat somewhere where they have a truly gaudy neon sign, so we drive around until we spot a place called "Rory's Rib Round-Up," with a picture of a cowgirl lassoing dogies out front. We get barbecue sauce all over us while she tells me how her Uncle Aloysius once lit his hair on fire trying to fry ants with a magnifying glass, and I tell her how my mom put mashed potatoes on her nose at the dinner table when nobody was paying attention to her. I pay the bill, but she leaves the tip. I enjoy being allowed to treat her this time. She can treat me back another night. It's a promising way to become indebted.

She mentions she's never seen a karate movie in her life, but on our way to a Bruce Lee triple feature at the drive-in, we stop to play a quick round of mini-golf for a dollar a hole, and while we're there, we run into a guy from the eight hundred eighty-seventh airborne, who tells us they're having a reunion at the Elks Club and we're invited since we seem like a nice couple, so we go and spend an entire evening listening to a fascinating old man tell stories about World War One while the dance floor thunders from the weight of big wives in mu-mus and men in uniforms that don't fit anymore, dancing to the polka sounds of Carmine Potretsky and His Accordionaires, ending with a sing-along medley that starts at "The Battle of New Orleans" and finishes with "When the Saints Come Marching In."

Which is only to say, my perfect date will be spontaneous, creative, unpredictable, open-minded, subject to change; won't take herself or the occasion too seriously; will include me in on whatever fun she finds in whatever we do; wants to know me; wants me to know her; isn't trying to impress me and so impresses me all the more; and has a feel for the flow of the evening. A perfect date is something you are, not something you do.

Who cares what you can *buy*? There are as many nice times to be had in Laundromats as there are in swank restaurants with multilingual busboys, as long as you're both equally involved in the date. Some men want to be in charge, but I just want to be joined, met halfway by a co-conspirator. That way, when my date and I kiss good night, it won't be because that's the traditional coda to the traditional evening. We'll do it because we've inspired each other to. That's what makes me want to call someone back.

Shopping

•

Receiving a gift of clothing from a girlfriend makes me nervous. It's not at all that I worry that I'll have to pretend to like something I don't and wear it for her once before throwing it out. It's more that I began to notice, sometime in my early twenties, that every time a girlfriend gave me clothes for a birthday or for Christmas or just for fun, shortly thereafter she told me she wanted to break up. At first I thought it was a curious coincidence, explicable according to Jung's theory of synchronicity and the collective unconscious, until, after the sixth or seventh time it happened, I arrived at a simpler explanation. Girlfriends give boyfriends clothes before dumping them to replace what they already know they're going to steal from him and probably have already set aside. They just want to be fair.

Still, we have to shop for each other. My attitude toward shopping has changed in recent years. I used to hate it. I had a drawer full of out-of-style pants that didn't fit because I couldn't stand to try them on in the store. I only shopped when I was home for Christmas and my mother made me go buy something with her credit cards. She buys things for my brother and sister, who stayed near home, and feels guilty when her generosity gets unevenly spread around. I've never had the kind of job where you have to impress people with your attire (come to think of it, I've never had the kind of job where you have to leave your house) and wear navy pinstripes and power ties, so I always figured I'd rather spend my money on things I could put in me than on me—beer, good food, maybe a movie or three. My attitudes toward fashion and style were largely informed by a sort of class consciousness, a deeply ingrained dislike of "pretty boys" who, when I was growing up, were generally rich kids who thought they were cool and who had a right to because they were, because their parents bought them all the trendy clothes they ever wanted, like Beatles jackets or madras Gant shirts with the loop on the back, not to mention expensive skates, bicycles, baseball mitts, and incredibly realistic battery-operated toy rifles that made gunlike noises and shot sparks out the barrel. Ooooh I hated those guys. And their clothes.

I mellowed on the subject when I moved to Rhode Island, where I taught writing at an art school and lived among Italians. Nobody celebrates style and looking good like Italians—I bought my first black shirt because of them. The art students carried self-decoration to extremes undreamed of in my native Midwest. The main look for men at the time was modeled after one of the school's most famous alumni, David Byrne, of the Talking Heads, the baggy camp look with cultural asides like string ties and a lot of black, and everything with paint smears here and there, even if you were a sculptor. Some weren't sure if they were real artists or not, and hoped that dressing like one would help make them one, but many were truly creative, and either way, the level of style in the community was so high that even I began to flash a little.

When I shop for myself, I still think of comfort first, soft fabric that doesn't cling. Banking and the legal profession are both out for me because you have to wear suits. I want clothes that are well made and will last a long time, Pendleton wools or L. L. Bean canvas shirts, Irish sweaters, good rayon. No polyester. I'd buy a Wayne Newton album first. I want to look warmly dressed when it's cold out and cool when it's hot, dry when it's raining. People who grew up in Minnesota's climate have a saying: "Live hard, die old, and leave a sensible-looking corpse." I'd rather look boyish than fancy—so far, anyway—but I'd also rather look sexy than sloppy.

I enjoy shopping with women, but I know men who don't, guys

who hate to shop, period. Except for stocking up for a fishing trip or buying new bats for the softball team, men don't shop with men. None of my buddies has ever called me and said, "Hey man, I gotta go pick up some new boxer shorts—wanna come?" We might brag later about what we bought ("Check out these polka dots"), but in the act of purchasing, we prefer to keep our consumption as inconspicuous as possible.

I really don't know too many women who feel the same way, part of why I'm so fond of shopping with them: I get vicarious pleasure from their pleasure. A friend worked in a small-town clothing store where the owner had to stay abreast of the current social circles and make sure not to sell the same dress to two women who knew each other or were likely to show up at the same party. The owner also had to remember what the women of the town tried on so that when their husbands came in later she could tell them what to buy. Women would come in and try things on for hours, preening in the mirrors, test-driving the merchandise the way men shop for cars. In big stores or major malls, women's departments or shops outnumber men's departments twenty to one. To me it seems so natural to shop with women. It was always my mother, never my father, who took the kids downtown on the bus to shop for school clothes. She knew where everything was—all I had to do was say what I wanted and she'd take me there. I was shocked, the first time she failed. I was about eight, and my favorite television show was "The Avengers," in which John Steed, the hero, an Englishman, wore double-breasted suits, bowler hats, and carried an umbrella. I wanted more than anything to wear double-breasted suits and bowler hats and carry an umbrella (and hear passersby go, "Look at that dapper eight-year-old!"), but somehow we couldn't find them anywhere. I still get the sense, because of my childhood training, that women know what they're doing in a large department store more than I do. When I'm shopping with a woman, I'm being given a guided tour through a foreign land. I regress in time, shrink from view.

In one sense, it's almost like I'm not there. She will keep an eye on me to make sure I don't get lost or knock something over, but beyond that, her attention is focused on the merchandise more. She accelerates toward the shoe department, braking sharply to examine a linen suit or two, then veers right toward the sweaters without signaling, slaloming deftly through the racks, hurdling parked baby strollers, making split-decisions at every aisle and counter. My place is ten feet behind. I keep up only slightly better now than I did as a boy trailing behind my mother, afraid of being abandoned. I've learned not to say anything committal when my opinion is asked for. My function is to be a sounding board, and it would be a big mistake if I tried to be something more. For one thing, I've never seen a woman try on anything I didn't like—if it's not at least a little bit right for her, she won't even pause to consider it. For another thing, I've never known anything I've ever said to make the slightest difference.

It's really a no-win scenario anyway. If a woman asks, "Does this make me look fat?" I'm not going to say yes. "How stupid do I look?" Don't answer that. And if she asks, which do I like, the blue one or the red one, I say, "They're both nice." Suppose I say I prefer the red. If she buys it and later hates the way it looks, I take the fall. If she buys the blue one and hates it, I'm to blame for not arguing strongly enough against it, or for the red. The only time I don't get credit is if she buys the red and likes it. The only thing I may say is, "Do you really need it?" I've gathered from all the cocked eyebrows I've received over the years that that's an irrelevant question. Now I ask, "How does it make you feel?"

I once did Harrods department store in London with a woman who had to have new shoes for the Exeter College Spring Ball, and we logged more miles in less time than any of the white-shorted runners in *Chariots of Fire*. I did shoes at Macy's with a friend who could sling plastic like Billy the Kid slung guns, venturing boldly forth into debt (the VISA zone) with an élan Captain Kirk from "Star Trek" would admire. One spring, I followed a woman through half the stores in Brazil and watched her spend enough money to rescue single-handedly the Brazilian economy from default. No matter where I've been or with whom, one thing has remained constant: the phrase "Watch my purse." I like this, too. I'm really good at it. I've never dropped or misplaced one. It's like Lady Godiva saying, "Hold my horse," or Cleopatra handing me the painter to her barge. I'm an attendant. Glad to be one. It makes me feel important.

I lived with a woman who owned so many clothes we considered moving into the closet and using the rest of the apartment for wardrobe. Though it's no longer trendy, her specialty was shopping thrift shops, places that would be reduced by fire to millions of coat hangers floating like twigs on oceans of melted polyester—yet nine times out of ten she could walk into one of them and find, within five minutes, a flawless fifteen-dollar fur coat or a six-dollar beaded sweater no moth's tooth ever touched. I was more than impressed. We would shop for hours, shopping for shopping's sake. Once she tried on summer dresses in a boutique, and I sat on the couch by the mirror outside the dressing rooms, giving her my opinions. At the same time, there were other women, trying on see-through lightweight summer tops, usually without having any underwear on under them. They wouldn't go out that way on the street, but it was okay in the store. I felt like a dirty old man, enjoying the free voyeurism. When I went back the next day, I really felt like one, especially when they kicked me out.

I will buy a woman anything but underwear or shoes—shoes because she would have to try each pair on to make sure of the fit, and underwear because it's too embarrassing. I tried it once, pretty much accidentally, when I was walking down a street of storefronts and happened into one of those pre–Valentine's Day Men's Nights, with *live models*, at a French lingerie shop, pass to see what it was all about, strictly as a reporter, with the plan to mingle unobtrusively with the crowd. As soon as I walked in, I saw there was no crowd, I was the only one there, but by then it was too late. The saleswomen, two of them, revealed far less flesh than anything you'd see on any beach in the summer, but they were still wearing underwear, teddies and chemises, and it was just plain strange to talk to a saleswoman wearing only underwear. Furthermore, they were clearly working on commission—I hadn't had such a hard sell since my local Subaru dealer broke down in tears and begged me to tell him what it would take to sell me a car. The taller saleswoman immediately asked to help me. "What's her size?" she wanted to know. "What does she like?" (Meaning what?) She followed me closely. "Would she wear this . . . or how about this? This one's very sexy—would you like me to try it on for you?" I hadn't blushed like that since a busload of Catholic schoolgirls caught me picking my nose at a red light. She kept positioning herself between me and the door, knowing no doubt that I would have had a hard time elbowing my way past a total stranger wearing only underwear. I faked left toward the cantilevered brassieres, and then, when she went for it, cut right around the Frederick's of Hollywood rack, and barely made it out the door, past the second saleswoman, who reached out from behind the cash register to stop me.

All I know is that I enjoy shopping with women. I like the way a woman will run her fingers along a seam, or scratch the fiber with a thumbnail to see if it's going to pull. I like the way she'll hold a blouse up with one hand, smoothing it out with the other, or try to tuck the hanger under her chin and talk to me at the same time without letting the hanger fall. I like to see what aesthetic decisions she makes, and then try to guess why she made them. I like to see her face light up with pleasure when she's found something that's just perfect for her. I empathize with her when she tries on something beautiful she can't afford and has to put it back.

If I watch closely and make mental notes, it's also the best way to know what to buy her when it's time to shop for her instead of with her. In China they have whole stores with nothing but black pajamas, and all a man has to know is her pajama size. It's easier, but then again, how often do Chinese women say, "Gee, black pajamas—how did you know?" In America there are thousands of ways a man can go wrong, apart from size, giving something too preppie, too yuppie, too freaky, too tacky, too trendy, or not trendy enough. The only sure bet is to give a woman the exact same thing she tried on four months earlier, fell in love with, and totally forgot about. "Gee, how did you know?" she'll say. "I got lucky," I say modestly.

Don't Undress Me
with Your Eyes

■

The party was an important one. It kicked off fall semester of graduate school, and so it was the first chance for second-year students to check out the new kids. I was a new kid, going for my M.F.A. in creative writing.

Among the second-year women were a poet and a novelist, both of them very modern, as my grandfather might have said, and aggressive. They were not afraid to look men in the eye. They were not afraid to look men in the lap either. Each had a corner of the room staked out, catching the men in a come-hither crossfire. I wasn't the only man who noticed. There were several of us, crawling across the living room floor on our stomachs to duck fire. We talked about it. It made all of us feel funny, not necessarily self-conscious, but more like we were being judged and sorted through. Who did they think they were? Of course, we'd judged women on their appearances ourselves. Was this how it made them feel?

We are all visual stimuli to one another, like it or not, objects to be observed until we actually meet and get to know each other. Traditionally, men have been the ones who did the looking, whistling, winking, and hooting. Now the tables are turning. Women can watch men all they want, buy "Buns" calendars or posters of a shirtless Don Johnson.

How does all of this make men feel? I, for one, enjoy being watched—most of the time. It's harmless, free, and it doesn't pollute the environment. It's a validation, like the day I stopped fighting my curly hair and started wearing it natural, only to see, for the first time in my life, girls actually peeking out of the corners of their eyes at me and smiling. It's nice to be looked at. Sometimes I'll do it up and hit the town in search of nothing more, really, than sideways glances. It makes my day, particularly when that day has been spent at home alone and I've begun to feel I've turned invisible. If I'm going out with my girlfriend, I'll dress just to see if I can get her face to light up the way it did when we first met. I like fishing for compliments almost as much as I like fishing for fish.

I don't like being watched when I feel my looks are being given more importance, for or against, than they warrant. I was once vamped at, Mae West style, by a woman I'll call Lola, whom I might have liked, had she not sidled up to me, ogling smugly with a sort of I'm-a-woman-of-the-eighties-and-I-get-what-I-want look on her face, to which I responded with my best oh-the-hell-you-do face. She made me feel I was being ranked, stereotyped, and manipulated. "Come hither" is one thing; "Here, boy—heel" is another. Maybe some men want to be thought of as ready-to-go sex toys, but I found it unenlightened—insulting even. It was a question of power, really, more than any philosophical argument against being treated as a sex object or anything political. I felt challenged to assert myself, at some real instinctive or emotional level. Mailmen who smile at dogs get bit because baring teeth is an act of aggression to a dog, and maybe in the same way, "coming on strong" to a man, in a way that is traditionally masculine, excites a competitive response, whether it's the eighties, the fifties, or the Middle Ages. It's probably true that men will respond, as they always have, to a coy or demure smile, signaling submission, before he'll respond well to a calculating or designing smile, signaling aggression. Both are positive reactions, but I'd have to say there was something about the way Lola smiled that I didn't like.

When the reaction is negative, and I draw frowns instead of smiles, though, I feel worse. Suppose a woman checks me out and then by some subtle gesture (she holds her nose or pretends to stick a finger down her throat) tells me she disapproves. It's not simply that my looks are being rejected. I grew up striving to please and impress people with what I do, how I write, draw, hit a baseball, trying to win affection by being kind and thoughtful. It hurts not to be judged on these attributes. I'm not sure I'd rate my looks at much better than 5 percent of what I ever based my sense of self on. Remember, I grew up with what I considered Bad Hair, deeply resented guys whose hair looked effortlessly like the Beatles', and took solace in hoping other things about me were adequate or even praiseworthy, if my hair was not. I still take solace in these things when seeking the inner wherewithal to ignore cold shoulders, and I tell myself that there's no future in women who ignore 95 percent of me anyway.

That resentment and those defense mechanisms really come into play when I lose out to another guy. Let's say I'm at a party being attended by a Mel Gibson look-alike. He will be standing by the hors d'oeuvres, drawing oohs and aahs, trying to count up to three on his fingers but getting stuck because two looks like eleven. I'll be standing by the drapes, thinking, I can write better than he can, sing better, I'm funnier. . . . There's a kind of automatic list I run through, one that hasn't changed much since high school. I'll bet half the guys at any party are doing the same sort of thing. Over half. I'll bet every man has a similar list. While Mel stuffs his rugged visage with canapés, the other guys are mentally clinging to whatever it is they think (or hope) makes them equal, wishing it showed. Except for the fat bald guys in the plaid sportcoats with three hairs drawn across the top of their scalps who think they're just as handsome as Mel Gibson and could get any twenty-year-old girl at the party if they could just remember what goes into a Rusty Nail and the names of three rock stars popular after Ed Sullivan went off the air. Some men just don't own mirrors that show them what they look like. Either way, it's an understatement to say men have not really been brought up to believe our looks are as important as women are told theirs are. If being watched makes us think more about the way we look, we think, so what? Or at least I do, getting upset only when something that doesn't matter does.

Like, for instance, the times my girlfriend is doing the looking, not at me. At a party, she tells me she thinks the guy across the room is handsome. Usually, I politely agree or disagree—I can't exactly tell her she has no taste.

"He's okay," I say.

In my head, though, I'm trying to add it all up. I'm not jealous and don't feel inadequate, but I start to go through my list. Then an awful thought occurs to me. What if the hunk across the room is just as kind, thoughtful, funny, and caring as I am, *plus* he makes Mel Gibson look like Anthony Quinn's evil twin?

"He is, of course, a pig," I tell her. "Obviously a pretentious poser who beats his plants and sells crack to kittens and puppies."

"Now, Peter," my girlfriend tells me, "don't be jealous."

"I'm not being jealous," I tell her.

I'm not. I'm being childish. Childish is different. And I have to be childish. It's my only advantage over superhunks—lightning-quick petty defense mechanisms that make me endearingly human.

The Language of Love

∎

THE PARABLE OF HOUDINI'S MOTHER

in the time of great magic
Houdini's mother
had nothing up her sleeves
no delivery room mirrors
nothing but nurses
in fishnet stockings
and doctors in top hats and tails

she was a frail drink of water
containing a battleship of determination
steaming towards a birth
never before attempted

she asked for silence
the doctors levitated her
passed a brass hoop over her
as she began to contract and push
beneath the red satin drapery

it was a difficult birth
accompanied by monotonous music
she sweated rivers
similar to those in South America
and she writhed like an uncharmed snake

until suddenly
with great flourish
the doctor raised high
from between her wet thighs
a bouncing seven pound
white rabbit

as the hospital gasped
a baby was heard to cry
from inside a padlocked cabinet
in the next room

so Houdini entered the world
with much applause
and no explanation
so too love enters the world
mothered of magic
somewhere quite other
than the pain and labor
it is delivered up in

if you don't believe me
you can look it up
when the secrets of love are published

I wrote that when I was twenty-six. I believed then, and I still
believe, that love is magical, surprising, and not gotten at directly.
Men and women do not go straight at love—they sidle up to it
obliquely. Our courtship strategies are probably more complicated,
not less, than those of goonie birds or bumblebees, the lower crea-

tures who strut and puff and make goofy noises and wiggle their heinies at each other. As higher creatures, we do all of the above (stick *Saturday Night Fever* in your VCR and you'll see what I mean) but go much further. We have the gift of speech, and so, in the early stages of courtship, we also use verbal dances, delicate linguistic maneuvers. The fine threads in the web we spin when we want to catch someone.

It's not dishonesty, so much as a kind of polite ambiguity, which lets you be straightforward and indirect at the same time. Our mating etiquette seems to insist on this approach. Too much initial directness may preempt other people's feelings and impose requirements on them before they're ready, scaring them off. Until you're able to be relaxed and candid with each other, being too matter-of-fact robs the situation of its romance.

I couldn't say I've ever really fallen for a woman solely on the basis of what she says, but I do sift through her words. I am vigilant in the first few conversations or dates, and there are particular things I look for.

First I look for interest, in who I am, what I do, and where I've been. I read a portion of my novel once to a woman, who said, "I could listen to you read to me forever." That's the best thing you can say to a writer, though you'd better laugh when you say it to show you're not serious, because most writers will be ready to take you up on it. The perfect thing to say will vary from man to man, but if you're really interested in a man, listen closely to him and you'll probably think of the right thing to say. Most people, I have learned, would rather talk about themselves than listen to someone else do so, since even chronically shy people have stories—everyone is looking for an opening, an ear. Listening, accepting someone's verbal offerings, is accepting him, and it feels good. Without trying to be self-centered (often I don't have to try), I love to be interrogated. It makes conversation so easy, because what I have to say is being sincerely sought. I am also usually aware, down to the minute, of how long I talk to people who don't ask me anything about myself, and keep sort of a running total in my head of how many questions I've asked them, and how many they've asked me.

I don't have to be the center of attention, but I'm not just standing there to be someone else's audience either.

After I feel that someone's interested in me, then I look for prospect, long and short term. I do this because, basically, I want to see as far into the future as I can, as soon as I can, so I may reach conclusions and make decisions. Short term means something fun is immediately possible, as in, "If you help me move my piano, I'll cook you dinner." Maybe it's a line, but though I'm wary of being manipulated, I'd leap at the chance to feel useful and needed.

A statement suggesting good long-term potential might be, "One day I want to have kids." I do too, one day. This may not work with a number of men, who would feel as if they're being sized up for fatherhood. If a woman were to say, "I don't ever want children," I would cut short any notion of a serious relationship then and there. I look for signs of sourness in spirit. A bad long-term statement might be, "I can't wait to get out of this town." After all, I live here and I'm staying.

Then I look for a level of affinity. There's almost a dating patter that begins, "Don't you just love/hate . . .?" I hate overhead lighting and cheap extension cords. I love ladies in their fifties who play the accordion, watching eighth-graders flirt in video parlors, and singing old TV theme songs. I like stories and am a sucker for women who know good ones, appreciate the bizarre or the ironic, someone who had an uncle who knew a guy who worked on an island off the coast of Maine where there were no phones, movies, TV, or electricity and that the movement on the island to keep it that way was being led by Thomas Edison's last surviving son. I look for affinity not just in what we like or know already but in how we're both curious, which would promise compatibility in both talking over the past and pursuing the future.

I also look for contrast, a degree of disaffinity. A woman once said to me, "I hate jokes," daring me to make her laugh. The tension set up by her challenge carried over and kept the relationship dynamic, after we'd reached a compromise. I could tell jokes, if she didn't have to laugh. Too much affinity is as bad as too little.

Then I look for sexual attraction. Not that I want to be propositioned, but I'd like it if a woman said, "What would you look like without a mustache?" or "Let me see your feet." I want to know there's a physical awareness there.

Finally, after I get an impression of someone's personality, and I know she's interested in me, and the match seems good, then I want to hear her comment on love itself. The woman who said she wanted me to read to her forever also said that love had disappointed her, and she didn't believe in it. I wanted someone who did and was sure of it. A woman I was wondering about courting once told me, not to entice me but just because we were talking about the subject, "I am so good when I'm in love, I just want to do everything for that person—you should see me."

Should see her? I *had* to. With a line like that? How could I resist? I didn't try. We were soon crazy about each other. I eventually wrote the "Parable of Houdini's Mother" for her, my way of trying to tell her that I couldn't really tell her adequately, with words, how I felt about her, that in the end the real language of love is nonverbal.

The Look of It

.

I sometimes think that if I could only watch a twenty-four-hour videotape of myself going through a normal day, I might finally know myself. People have always wondered what it would be like to see themselves as others do, but a videotape would be enormously satisfying to the superego, the part of the consciousness that watches the other parts. You could freeze-frame at the high points, rerun the confusing parts in slow motion, and fast-forward through the parts where you embarrass yourself. I'm sure I could watch myself trip on a set of stairs over and over and still find a way to deny it and tell myself I'm generally graceful, but then again, maybe I'd understand why everyone always assumes I'm grumpy or cross when in fact I feel fine, what exactly my Norwegian scowl (a face first worn by Viking sailors when they thought they were about to sail their long dragon ships off the edge of the world but weren't about to turn around even if they were, now appearing on the visages of Scandinavians everywhere) actually looks like to strangers.

I'd really be interested to watch myself fall in love, what signals I give, how much my self-consciousness shows. Maybe it could be one of those instructional films, to show in girls' health classes in high school, *Pete Falls in Love*, with an introduction by Whitney Houston singing "How Will I Know If He Really Loves Me?"

The movie opens with me in the shower, putting conditioner on my hair. I usually just shampoo, but this is a big day. I know something extraordinary is happening to me, but I keep telling myself to behave as though things are business as usual. Even so, I forget to put money in parking meters and lose my place reading the paper. I will leave a message on your answering machine and then check back ten minutes later to be sure you got it. I call frequently, but I have absolutely nothing to say. I might even concoct implausible excuses to be "in the neighborhood," or "just stopping by." I once noticed a girl's toothbrush was worn and bought her a new one to have a reason to come by and see her. Then I just stood there, watching her fold laundry, enjoying every minute of it. "Men in love," the narrator says, "are easily amused."

We go on a date. I might betray myself in a number of ways. If I'm picking you up in my car, observe the angle of the rearview mirror. If the first thing I do is adjust it more than a few inches, you know I was checking myself in it one last time, looking for anything about my appearance that might embarrass me, like little pieces of toilet paper I've forgotten to remove from my shaving wounds. The gas gauge says the tank is full because I want to be ready, in case we both decide to dash madly off for a romantic weekend.

"Nobody pulls the 'we're out of gas' stunt anymore," the narrator says. "If he does, tell him you want to throw a match down the tank, just to be sure. He'll get the point."

At dinner, if I'm really in love, I will wear my best clothes, but all the same, I will probably be nervous and spill something on myself, if not on you. I'll have a predinner drink to calm myself, probably order wine with the food and pretend I know something about it though when I eat alone I never touch the stuff. I'll have coffee afterward to stay alert.

During the course of the evening there would be considerable laughter and extensive eye contact, though I will also examine every square inch of you, not out of lust, but to take in and record all of you, noticing your posture, how your toes point when you sit, hoping to sate an insatiable desire to know you better.

If you come back to my apartment, look for signs of excessive fastidiousness. The camera pans. Is the kitchen floor waxed? "Men will not wax floors," the narrator intones, "unless someone im-

portant is coming over whom they want to impress." Is the toilet
seat down for you? If I have an address book, have I written your
name in it in ink? Have I stocked things men have no use for—
vitamin E creams, Diet Cokes, cotton balls, and so on? Are the
sheets changed? The dog washed and combed? No dishes in the
sink, or even in the drying rack? Magazines in which I've published
strewn casually about where you can see them? Do I smile and
look goofy because I know I'm about to say something along the
lines of "I love you," as if the feeling were uncontainable?

We embrace. Cut to ocean waves crashing on the shore, sunset,
and then an owl winking right at the camera.

The music accompanying the film *Pete Falls in Love* will under-
score my sincerity. There's a jump cut to a slick-looking dude in
a Corvette convertible with a terrified-looking girl in the seat beside
him. "Beware of imitation," the narrator says. "There are men
who are not in love but merely in lust, who say 'I love you' knowing
all the while they don't mean it." The music becomes evil, something cold in a minor key, and the movie shows the slick dude
doing things to indicate that he not only takes love lightly but takes
other important things lightly too. He drives irresponsibly and be-
haves inconsiderately in public, both to his date and others. He
smokes in no-smoking areas and walks so fast the girl can't keep
up. He doesn't look her in the eye to see who she is, so much as
he looks to gauge what effect he's having. He talks about himself,
without being asked to, going light on the apologies and heavy on
the alibis. "Men in lust are full of themselves," the narrator says.
"Men in love are full of you."

Dissolve to Whitney Houston sitting at a soda fountain, sipping
Diet Coke. Some handsome guy comes over, kisses her on the neck,
and then leaves. She turns to the camera and says, "So remember,
girls—if he acts confused and kind, nervous and bold, foolish and
earnest, but, above all, happy, chances are it's the real thing for
him. Of course, getting a lot of 'go' signals isn't always good news,
because then you have to decide if it's real for you too."

Of course, I have no such video. I do have an old photograph,
taken one of the times when I was falling in love, in which my

girlfriend and I are standing outside a restaurant in the snow, with our arms around each other. We had the waitress take it. When I'm in love, my smile looks natural, not manufactured for the camera, and it covers my whole face. I lean ten degrees from vertical toward the woman I'm in love with. I do romantic, silly things, like having a waitress take our picture. I look pretty happy. My girlfriend looks a little worried, though.

Practical Romance

■

Mothering/Smothering

■

Parenting for each other in a relationship, or being the strong one when the other person wants to be the weak one, doing for your beloved and taking care of him or her is a nice service to provide for each other, especially since we learn how to be in love, doubtless more than many of us want to admit, from our own parents. We learn as well what kind of affection or attention we need from them. My mother had a particular way of stroking my forehead when I was feeling low or blue that still calms me when my girlfriend does it. Smothering, unlike good mothering, is when you give someone more than they want to receive, more than they feel they need to be happy, that amount probably defined by the way they were raised. It can be like trying to pour a quart of milk into a pint bottle. All you get is a mess.

I recognized the need for a mother at an early age, when, a few hours old, I realized that I was quite hungry and that, brand new to the world, I had no idea where the closest restaurant was. And even if I found it, I didn't have any money either. My first major setback. So soon too. I opened my mouth and voiced my disappointment.

And there was food. And it was good.

I grew to trust the huge, soft person who followed me around, and kept going, "Can you say 'Mama'?" She taught me simple, elemental things I still find useful. How to find my toes. How to keep my head from wobbling. Over the years, I learned how to blow my own nose and make my own way. In high school, she declared war on my personal sense of style, issuing endless unreasonable demands to pick up my clothes, make my bed, quit smoking, stop stealing cars. It put some distance between us. By the time I reached college, though I found it handy to Federal Express my dirty laundry home from time to time (please bill recipient), I nevertheless considered myself completely weaned. On my own. Joe Tough Guy.

Halfway through my freshman year, I got sick. Just a forty-eight-hour bug, with a low fever. I was totally miserable. My friends showed no sympathy whatsoever. I couldn't go see Dr. Put-a-cast-on-it at the infirmary. There's hardly as forlorn a feeling as being sick away from home for the first time. Who'd take my temperature, bring me ginger ale, stroke my forehead, and tell me not to worry? I wanted my mommy.

It's no secret that men are not as tough as we pretend to be. Any man who loves his mother will respond to mothering from his *significant other*. I'll bet even Mr. T wants a gal like Ma T, someone to tell him to hang up his jewelry and not growl with his mouth full. Of course, we're all agreed that there should be a mandatory death penalty for adults who talk baby talk to each other in public, but in private, or so long as you don't whine and kitchy-coo like twerps, why not parent a little?

Most men, I think, will have a sense of what "being the dad" might mean, stepping into old-fashioned traditional male roles like repairing things, doing the driving, acting strong when storms beset, whatever we learned from our fathers. It's just play-acting, but there's a sort of security in it, a feeling of continuity: "Here I am, chopping wood, just like the old man used to." Most of the women I've known seemed to have had a sense of what "being the mom" meant too, enjoying playing or parodying the same traditional roles, cooking up a big meal or showing me how to use the sewing machine. I in turn play the son, turn to the woman I love for succor and solace, a bosom to bury my face in, a benevolent female to confess to and depend on. We indulge each other, trade the position of authority back and forth, granting it or assuming it.

Smothering is different. Smothering has the word "mother" in it only accidentally. What it means is to suffocate. I know a woman who gets up every morning at six to iron her husband's shirts. If my wife did that, I'd divorce her just as soon as she was finished. But seriously, it's no joke to say excess is as bad as neglect. It's another case where the golden rule is a real bum steer. Maybe you want to love someone, give to him, and care for him in exactly the way you want to be loved, given to, and cared for. That's fine, but then again, who are you to presume the other person feels exactly the way you do? The rule only works in the negative: don't do to others what you don't want done to you. In the positive, try to intuit what the other person wants done and then do that, which in some cases may not be having all his shirts ironed.

Everyone wants love, but everyone also wants, some of the time, to be allowed a certain amount of private territory, just as everyone had a shoebox in the closet where their mother was not welcome. Excessive mothering makes me feel like my shoebox is in jeopardy. It feels like nervous love, or at least if a woman did it to me, I'd find it hard not to suspect the motivation behind it—is she insecure? When I'm fretful or insecure about a relationship, that's what I do, buy flowers, try extra hard to think of fun things to do, try extra hard to be nice or attentive just because I'm worried. Is she afraid something is wrong? Is she trying to make up for something? Is she trying to buy my love? Is this a subtle guilt trip she's laying on me, a mounting debt she'll ask me to repay some day? Is she trying to get something from me? If I'm being paranoid or taking it wrong, then it's another twist on the golden rule: don't assume someone who does what you do has the same reasons.

I don't know quite how to tell where it is, but there is, all the same, a point past which doing nice things for your other is counterproductive. It's okay for you to ask me if I've gained a little weight, but don't secretly prepare diet meals for me. Say, "That color looks good on you," but not, "That shirt's all wrong on you—

let *me* pick something out." I'm thirty-five. I can dress myself. Tell me you wish I'd quit smoking, but don't hide my cigarettes. Give me some credit, and give me enough room to love you back, without trying to impose your love on me or demand mine.

It is hard to tell someone when they've crossed the line from mothering to smothering. It can easily feel as if one person is saying, "I want to love you," but the other person is saying, "Well, I don't want you to." It seems that people try to give each other signals before it becomes a big issue. I might say, "Thanks, but you don't really have to do that." I mean, "Please, don't do that." If it's hard not to give someone all the love you feel, it's also true, as most mothers learn after the boy grows up, that you can love by letting go. Easier said than done, to trust it, trust him (or her), trust yourself, really, and be cool about it, let go a little if the other person asks you to. Maybe it's more useful to think of *letting* someone be happy, rather than making him happy. At the same time, you want to be allowed to love the way you know how. Some people match up from the start, while others take years to adjust to each other. All you can do is try to stay alert and sensitive to the signals when someone says, "Back off." If they're saying they're satisfied already, maybe you can find some satisfaction in that as well.

The only time when I really want to be smothered is when I'm sick. Some people want to be left alone when they're sick, allowed to hole up in a cave somewhere, crawl off into the brush to lick their wounds. Not me. I warn people right up front that when my temperature goes over 100, I turn ten again, get totally weepy and emotional, and start playing for all the sympathy I can get, because when I'm sick, I want it all. I want juices, sponge baths, back rubs, medicine (and of course I will gladly administer all of the above in return if the situation is ever reversed), and even then, I want something else. I want the phone near the bed, so I can call my mother.

Even smothering only goes so far.

Amorophobia

■

Darryl Dawkins, the pro basketball player, was once asked by a reporter, "Darryl, you're six feet eleven, two hundred fifty pounds—tell me, is there anything you're afraid of?"

"Well," Dawkins is said to have replied, "the only thing I'm afraid of is the unknown. That, and ice skating."

I am not afraid of ice skating. I'm only a little afraid of Darryl Dawkins. On occasion I have been terrified of the unknown. There may be a real word for it, but I call the fear of love "amorophobia," which, like any other neurosis, is a fear that a huge force beyond your control is going to destroy you. Got it? Welcome to the planet.

For me, it starts on the fourth date, or as soon as I know enough about someone to say to myself, "Oh my God—this person is wonderful and perfect. There's nothing whatsoever wrong with her, and we get along great. She's the kind of person I could conceivably marry." You'd think this would be good news, and it is; but from here on, a kind of panic sets in. Think of the power over your life you hand someone, when you decide to love her. Can't be, I say. There must be a way out. I search for hidden, fatal flaws. I start to blow small, insignificant incompatibilities out of proportion. "It'll never work," I tell myself. "She likes cats and I'm allergic." Or "It's over—she likes to dance and I have a bad knee."

Why should I be afraid of what I want? Probably because all of my adult life, I've pursued successful love and sought to acquire something deep and lasting and wonderful, which is entirely dif-

111

ferent from actually having it. I'm fairly well acquainted with doomed relationships. I feel at home in them. But suppose I get what I've always wanted. Then what happens? Who am I then, since I can't be who I've always been anymore? And what am I half of? It's the curse of imagination to have premonitions of disaster, but that's what mine does. What if I blow it? I've blown it before. What if I'm wrong? What if she changes? What if I change?

If you think about it, it all boils down to the fear of losing control over your life and your destiny. Men with chronic amorophobia flee change and return it to the safe, solitary life, which is the one they're familiar with, if not comfortable with.

How can you help a man to take a chance on love? If he's been skirting the commitment issue for a while, it might be time to find out where and how he lost faith in love, or, more to the point, in himself. I don't think you should press him about it, though, or turn push into shove—just address the fears. Maybe the best way to get him to open up is to talk about your failures and heartaches, your own dashed expectations and why they were so high in the first place. Talk about doubt and why it seems to increase with age—not diminish. Then talk about how people really do grow to fit each other, without losing your old selves—so people who are happily married will tell you. And what the hell, you could offer him a substitute for his fear of commitment, like the fear of going through the rest of his life alone or even the fear of contracting sexually transmitted diseases ranging from gross to fatal.

Mention, as well, that two can live more cheaply than one (though for only half as long). Personally, I'm starting to think I'm too old not to be divorced at least once yet. People have begun to make fun of me.

Maybe fear of love is just a phase of love, a rock along the path toward commitment. A cautious coming around, which is the way human beings bargain with most major changes in life. Ultimately, a leap of faith is in order, an act of believing that the bargain is good and will last; that love, which has the power to destroy, will create instead. It's a push out from shore, a belief that the ice will hold.

Humor in Bed

.

I saw a bumper sticker once, borrowing from *Annie Hall*, that read: SEX IS THE MOST FUN YOU CAN HAVE WITHOUT LAUGHING.

Sez who? Sex without humor? If I wanted humorless sex, I'd date Queen Victoria, who is dead, but not as dead as a humorless love life would be. They say people do not (because they cannot) laugh about the things they find truly threatening. I would find someone who couldn't laugh about sex a little scary.

I should admit I may not be the most objective person in the world when it comes to humor. There's the old joke where a king tells his court jester, whom he'd sentenced to hang for his bad puns, that he won't hang him if the jester promises not to pun again, to which the jester replies, "Well, no noose is good news," and swings for it. Sometimes I feel a little like that jester, prone to making jokes when I shouldn't, but I can't help myself. Once I was lying in bed with a woman with whom I was falling head over heels in love, and vice versa. We were holding each other in the quiet afterglow of lovemaking, and she was expressing the kinds of feeling you only talk about in quiet afterglows, how she'd never felt this way before, how surprised she was, what it was exactly about me that she loved so much, her hopes, her fears, for ten or fifteen straight minutes, how nothing had ever felt so right, how I was different from any man she'd ever met, and that her only worry was that I might not love her back as much as she loved me. What did I think? she asked.

113

I paused.

"I'm sorry—what were you saying?" I said.

Maybe you had to be there. We're glad you weren't, but we certainly chuckled and guffawed.

A relationship without humor is sort of like being fed intravenously. Sure it's a form of sustenance, but I want to taste love and savor it. I couldn't have a relationship with a humorless woman, even if she looked like Rosanna Arquette and was heir to a huge family fortune. After a few years, it just wouldn't work. It's the woman I've joked with at a party, felt at ease with, that I want to invite home. Maybe sex is the most fun you can have without laughing, but to me, laughing is the most intimate thing two people can do together without having sex. In public, anyway.

In private, there's another thing they can do, but humor should be a part of that, too—the one almost an extension of the other. It's called fore*play*, not fore*work*. This is not the time to tell bad jokes, but you don't want to be deadly serious either. If it's your first time together, you can't help feeling nervous. A little jocularity can relieve the tension. If you're old lovers, humor can restoke the fire, one way to keep the experience fresh and new. A laugh is the most authentic expression anyone can make—you want to be authentic with each other, don't you? It's also one of the friendliest. It can be very seductive, since you both know there is soon going to come a point, after foreplay, where you may want to stop laughing.

That's a point you don't want to misjudge. Lovers tell each other, usually more by gesture than by word, when it's time to, well, bear down, cut the horsing around. You can hurt someone's feelings by seeming less involved than he is. I was with a woman once who kept giggling about a joke I'd told her long after I'd stopped feeling like laughing. Maybe it was nervous laughter on her part, or maybe I was being impatient, but one thing was evident—we were not on the same wavelength.

Afterward, though, everything seems absurdly risible and good. We often lie there giggling at the good thing we did. When all defenses are dropped and there's nothing left to prove, I can bare more of my soul, confess things in what is almost a childlike intimacy, a kindergarten sleepover goofiness. This is the time to play footsie, give funny names to rarely personified body parts, play motorboat or Mr. Microphone, even explore the world of silly kissing with or without mouth noises.

You do need to be careful about some of the jokes you make in bed. While people may be more open with each other there, they may be more sensitive too. Once, just after we'd made love, my girlfriend wondered aloud if one of her closest friends was "easy." I jokingly asked her, "Want me to sleep with her to find out?" That's when I learned an important thing about my girlfriend: threatening her with infidelity was not likely to amuse her, even when said in jest. Making the same wisecrack during dinner might have gone over. In bed, it did not.

All in all, the way you share your time before and after sex is what elevates it above the merely physical. Laughter is proof, just as sex is, that you really do enjoy each other's company. I wouldn't put much stock in a relationship in which the man and woman don't like to horse around with each other. In fact, the best couples I know are the ones that have private jokes between them. Love is not a joke, nor need you be eternally cheerful to have a good relationship. It's just that I remember the nights we had each other in stitches longer than I do the nights we simply had each other.

Birth Control

■

It was the first time I'd ever eaten steak grilled over mesquite coals. The word "yuppie" had not yet been invented. The air was hot and dry, and the sunsets got redder every day. It was spring. I was living in the desert town of Tucson, and so was Julia. Julia and I had a month to go before we were both moving to different cities, at opposite ends of the universe. She was going to Africa, in fact, I to Iowa. A gentle, sweet affair was how we wanted to spend the time left. This was our first night, and it was memorable. It was the first time I ever encountered a diaphragm, or as it's popularly known, the "despised trampoline of love."

Before then, I never knew or cared about them, or, for that matter, about any of the other forms of birth control. None of my business, I figured. When Julia jumped out of bed, *in medias res*, as it were, and ran to the bathroom to install her diaphragm, it became my business. It was as if, in the middle of a symphony, the conductor took a coffee break, leaving the orchestra to tune their instruments. The melody lingered on, but the song was gone, at least for that night.

I'm older and wiser now. Even so, orchestrating birth control has not gotten any easier, for me or for anyone else I know. Sometimes soaringly passionate relationships can swoon down in a spiral of diminishing returns, when the trouble of preparing for sex is greater than the reward of doing it.

Things were simpler in the sixties, the Golden Age of Contraceptive Innocence before we found out the Pill wasn't necessarily

116

the blessing it first appeared to be. It made sex easy. It gave women a greater degree of control over their sexuality. Everyone could have pleasure without consequence. Before the Pill, being "casual" about sex meant you were loose and immoral; after it, it meant you were free, spiritually uninhibited, and, once the usage became common, it simply meant you were normal. In post-sexual-revolution hindsight, some people have come to think that having casual commitment-free sex may not have been the best way to spend their time. I know some women who feel misled or even betrayed by the "sexual revolution," as if the Pill were an invention men came up with to get more sex. They wouldn't say being kept barefoot and pregnant was better, but now they want something in between, with pleasure and romance and control over their sexuality, but with commitment and possibly a family too.

Men no doubt loved the Pill as much as women did, or more, since we weren't the ones getting sick from taking it. I was a mere boy at the time it was developed, and it wasn't common for teenage girls to take the Pill yet. It seemed to follow, therefore, that the ones who went first were the most eager, readiness being equated with willingness. All I knew was that it relieved me of having to go into a drugstore and buy condoms, an idea that terrified me. Seventy-five out of the first hundred dirty jokes I heard during puberty were about boys getting caught buying rubbers and being humiliated. For all the legends and stories of boys carrying rubbers in their wallets, I never did, and no one I ever knew showed me he did either. Maybe nobody told me anything, or maybe those stories are told by men a few years older than I was, and I stumbled into puberty at a time after the Pill came out but before the revolution really got going and the average age when people lost their virginity began to drop. The Pill, for my generation, meant birth control was the woman's responsibility, and I was glad of it, because I was so awkward about the whole business that I might have ended up one of those teenagers who make love without using contraceptives. A recent survey found that 56 percent of today's teenagers don't use anything the first time they make love just because they're too shy and embarrassed to talk about it.

In monogamous couples, men still, from fear, ignorance, awkwardness, or selfishness, prefer to let the woman "take care of it." It partly reflects the way we've been conditioned to think about sex that men are encouraged to sow the wild oats while women have been taught to be cautious; that we supply the drive, while you prepare for the consequences. I could be the second-most-sensitive guy in the world, right behind Michael J. Fox, and care as much as I possibly could about sharing contraceptive responsibilities with the woman I love, and the net sum of my concern would even so be less than hers. After all, she's the one who runs the risk of getting pregnant. We don't live with a daily awareness of the possibility, and can only imagine what it might be like. A man's main concern for birth control is with its intrusiveness. That's no small thing. A woman friend of mine and I concluded one night, after one of those long lubricated conversations where you solve all the mysteries of love over a glass of Jack Daniel's, that women were perhaps as concerned about getting pregnant as men are about failing in bed, which can be the result, I learned the night I had mesquite steaks, of the intrusion of birth control. For men, the humiliation of temporary impotence surpasses inconvenience.

Needless to say, everything has changed dramatically in recent years for nonmonogamous couples or for single people making love for the first time. The past is moot, now that birth is practically the least of the things about sex we worry about controlling. I think I read every newspaper article about AIDS from beginning to end, and I'm still not entirely clear on what the actual statistics are for contracting the disease through heterosexual activity. I try to console myself with other statistics, that it may be I'm still more likely to get hit by a truck and die than die of AIDS, but people are not biologically compelled to drive trucks (*most* people aren't), and the number of trucks on the road isn't doubling every year. I'm definitely paranoid, maybe just as unreasonably paranoid about the subject as the next guy, because I don't want to die any more than he does, but all the same I can't imagine acting as if there is no threat, as some people apparently still do, or really, acting as if the odds weren't 100 percent certain that everyone I could possibly sleep with has it, in which case there is no further argument over what form of birth control to use—the beloved condom.

I'm trying to think of a way to make it fun. I can't. Dr. Ruth says people should make putting the condom on part of the arousal process, but every time I try, I think of Dr. Ruth. Now it's gotten to where I can't even get halfway through a decent sexual fantasy without stopping, in the fantasy, to put a rubber on. Men hate rubbers, as the small turnout for the National Condom Week Parade testified (see, no one even remembers it). At best, it's an intrusion and an expense, but at worst, the condom has the reputation of feeling like petting a kitten with mittens on, showering in a raincoat, eating with a mouthful of novocaine. The reputation may be exaggerated, and perhaps the AIDS tragedy will get men over thinking of the condom as a nightmare and realize it really isn't that bad, that sex, even with a condom on, is still more fun than reading Longfellow or poking yourself in the eye. Now, of course, there are ads in women's magazines that will have the effect of making contraception the woman's responsibility again, not that it matters anymore, politically, who buys the rubbers or takes care of making sex safe. What matters is that the consequences are now so grave that men and women both have to be equally responsible for them. There may be a wholly different kind of pleasure to be found in facing that responsibility together.

Birth control never was a subject people felt fond or sentimental about, but it can be something two people share, part of the loving process. Women may need to initiate the discussion, given the history of men leaving it up to them, but I think most men would join in willingly, and be glad to have the subject out of the way. They are saying that people need more than ever to share their sexual histories before getting involved with each other, talk over the risks, and agree as to what to do about them. Birth control can be just another way of getting to know each other. Contraception is its own reward, once you get the hang of it, as Julia and I discovered, the month of the tasty steaks, back when the air was hot and dry, and the sunsets got redder every day.

Gentle Persuasion

■

My friend Reese married Cathy, a woman of great tolerance and considerable patience, which is lucky for both of them, because Reese is a man who once, in public, was heard to confess, "I still wear my bell-bottoms sometimes—they're really comfortable." Cathy rolled her eyes and looked heavenward, for the strength she'd need to face the task of changing Reese into someone she could be seen with in restaurants.

If nobody's perfect, then there's no such thing as the perfect mate, which is why most people usually compromise by finding someone who comes reasonably close and then correcting him. Others go even farther than that. I know guys who, taking it to the extreme, have what amount to Pygmalion complexes, the belief that you can completely remake a lover into a new person, a belief I'm sure some women share as well. I think it's a big mistake, or at least a bad bet, to enter into a relationship under any such premise, misled into involvement with someone you know "isn't your type," hoping she'll become your type. No one changes that much, and even if people do make a noble effort, they change back, sooner or later. I want to be taken *as is*, not made to feel there's something wrong with me (even if there is). I've known people who've bent over backwards to be what their mates want them to be, who've given up camping, taken up jogging, really tried to alter their personalities, but who then realize one day that bending over backwards is an unnatural position to put themselves in. They snap to, feel like themselves again, and can't imagine going back to what the relationship made them be.

It's also true that you have to compromise. People work on each other in subtle ways, consciously and unconsciously. We can't alter each other's personalities, but maybe we can take the rough edges off and smooth down the lumpy parts.

Take my appearance. Men frequently suffer from what a girlfriend once called "fashion disorders," and often love clothes more for sentimental or practical than artistic reasons. Wearing bell-bottoms for comfort in the 1980s makes perfect sense to Reese. I wasn't able to throw out an old pair of tennis shoes when I was five, thinking of all they'd meant to me, and I still can't. Don't try to argue taste with me, because you can't argue taste, and it'll just make me stubborn. I don't know why I hate purple—maybe I was chased in a dream by Goofy Grape when I was six—but buying me a purple shirt would be a waste of money. Nor would I like it if someone were to surreptitiously delete from my wardrobe those items whose time has gone. A friend of mine used to move her husband's bad shirts to the lower drawers or the ends of the closet rack, knowing that men with fashion disorders dress themselves from whatever is on top or easiest to reach. Maybe you can't argue taste, but you can perhaps affect it through flattery, which persuades better than criticism. I'd buy what a girlfriend admires before I'd forgo what she scorns.

I do respond to hygienic assistance. If my girlfriend were to make dental appointments for both of us, I'd go, as long as she goes too. And first. I defer to her regarding hair care as well, since there are shampoos for oily, dry, blond, dandruffy, or "sensitive" hair, but, in my neighborhood drugstore at least, surprisingly not a single one saying, "Special Formula for Men." I really don't care. If someone wanted to use a shampoo, she might tell me she likes the way it makes my hair *smell* and forget the rest.

Habitual behavior is tougher to change, but not impossible. The first time I quit smoking was for a woman. In fact, we were going to quit together, and ended up falling in love in the process. She kept smoking. I started again after that relationship ended and quit when my next girlfriend said, "If you die of cancer, I'll never come visit you in the hospital." If I'm eating or drinking too much, reminding me of the facts, the medical data, is usually enough to spur me toward improving myself.

What you can't change is the spirit that moves people, what they consider to be their nature. Someone who's been shy all his life won't turn suddenly gregarious when taken to a lot of parties, and someone who is chronically restless, like I am, won't calm down just by being told to. The trick is figuring what it is about the other person that makes him him, or her her, and then adjusting your own attitudes until you can accept that. Our flaws make us unique as much as anything.

One way to adjust is to teach yourself to enjoy what the other person enjoys. I've tried to like what my girlfriends have liked. I'd rather drink Drāno than go to the ballet—to me, the Lakers versus the Celtics is not only better dance, but it's better drama, because no one knows how it's going to end. Even so, when I dated a woman who always saw *The Nutcracker* at Christmas, we went, and I managed to stay awake through the whole thing, mostly by watching for someone to fall down. On my own, I would not attend a choral concert in a million years, or maybe that's too strong—in half a million years—just because I got dragged to so many of them against my will as a kid, but when I dated an alto in a chamber choral group, I not only went to her performances, but I surprised myself and found I sort of liked them.

I know I have some affections that my girlfriends have not shared.

I honestly like watching golf on TV. As a former summer hacker raised on par threes and public links, I can appreciate the skill of pros like Greg Norman or Jack Nicklaus. To someone who doesn't play golf, the game may look like an elaborate form of croquet played by rich white Anglo-Saxon Protestant men who can't dress themselves. It's an exercise in class voyeurism, though, like "Dynasty" or "Lifestyles of the Rich and Famous." Watching golf allows me to fantasize about owning the expensive things advertised during golf tournaments. And even on TV, the green grass and the warm sun can give one a sense of serenity, particularly when it's summer where they're playing and winter where you're watching. I go with the serenity. It usually leads to an afternoon nap, which is the real reason to watch televised golf, and something men and women can and should share.

I love baseball. The high moment of one relationship I had was taking my girlfriend to her first baseball game, a Red Sox game at Fenway Park. Actually, I told her "Fenway Frank" was the team mascot and "Seventh-Inning Stretch" was the nickname for the lanky Texan on the grounds crew who got a standing ovation whenever he came out to groom the base paths. Usually the women I've known have had a passion for baseball equal to mine. Men do have a slightly different take on the game, though. Many men harbor the secret fantasy that we, too, could have played pro ball. We remember one golden childhood moment, a great catch or a towering home run, and invent entire imaginary careers based on that one moment.

I like camping. I know lots of women who love camping too, but for some reason I've never dated any of them. I know it's hard to be enthusiastic when you're cold and dirty and mosquitoes big enough to fillet are making your blood the *soup du jour*. Couples who thought they were in love enough to survive twenty-five years of marriage have been known to go camping and emerge from the woods separately, days and miles apart, never to speak to each other again. Not everyone relishes hardship and deprivation equally. The trick to camping with anybody is, as they say in the Boy Scouts, to be prepared. I know I don't want to feel that someone I've lured into the wilderness is having a terrible time and it's my fault. Before embarking on a camping trip, know what to expect and then be *overprepared*. The person who still has mosquito repellent on the last night can even make a tidy profit.

Changing someone, or meeting him halfway, doesn't have to degenerate into a battle of egos or a struggle for power. In her book *Intimate Partners*, Maggie Scarf describes couples who become locked in a kind of "If you win, I lose" duel to the death, defending who they think they are, when the truth is that two people are either going to win or lose together. I wouldn't think too many relationships last when a person's whole sense of self is threatened by it, generating those absurd fights where someone yells, "Yeah, well, I've *always* put ketchup on my Grape-Nuts, so the hell with you!" Little things become huge when they're emblematic of your entire personality, when you're no longer defending the way you eat Grape-Nuts but really your right to exist as the same person you know you've always been. Those couples who seem to fit so irritatingly well together seem to know when to agree and when to let the other person go ahead and be wrong, while making honest efforts to respect and appreciate each other, even when they don't agree. Just by dint of living the example, people in love gently persuade each other, and change comes slow, something well-suited couples seem to know. Reese and Cathy look better together every time I see them, and Reese hasn't worn bell-bottoms in years.

Competing with a Man

■

I mopped the sweat from my brow and stood panting in the early evening sun, weary to the bone and completely vanquished. Across the court stood my friend Kari. She'd just beaten me, fair and square, 6–2, 6–2. Her passing shots were deft, and her drop shots had sent me sprawling with a mouthful of asphalt. Granted, she'd been the captain of her high school tennis team, and I'd never played all that much tennis, but I'd really thought I could beat her.

"Good game," I said.

"You too," she said. "We should play tennis again after they take this thing off." She pointed to the plaster cast covering her left leg. *Toe to hip.*

I could live with this loss, maybe because Kari and I were old friends and, therefore, I had nothing to prove to her, or maybe it was because I learned somewhere not to resent someone who beats you fair and square. I wasn't thrilled about it, but it was okay. There are men, though, who don't like losing to women, even if it is fair and square. How can a woman play games with a man and win, without fearing she'll upset him, lose his friendship, or even his love?

First you've got to realize that most men approach competition differently from most women. It is said that boys play competitively while girls play cooperatively. My sisters used to play office together, creating elaborate sets, with rules and titles and even props,

125

office supplies our father brought home from work. They'd have friends over, and everyone would take turns playing different roles in different constructions—a play school, a play office, a play hospital, or whatever.

Cooperation never worked that smoothly with boys. We tried forming what we called the Genius Club, a group of boys in the neighborhood which met once, long enough to build a clubhouse in our garage, but which broke up when we couldn't settle on who was the biggest genius or reach a consensus on a proposition, put forth by an older boy, that the younger boys had to pay dues but the older boys did not. Competition worked better. My brother and I simply tried to tear each other's head off wrestling, or put huge black-and-blue bruises on each other's shins playing golfball hockey in the sunroom. The more boys that competed, the more we liked it. There is no greater joy in a boy's heart than a playground victory. Conversely, there are no worse moments in boydom than losing a game, hearing the derision of a "Nyaah, nyaah, nyaah." The point is, males take games real seriously. "It's only a game" is a phrase coined to comfort losers. "It's more than a game" is what winners say. My coaches were always telling me that, that if I gave up and quit in the middle of pursuing some swift halfback around left end in a football game, later in life I'd be a quitter too, would end up a degenerate drug addict. In fact, it was mostly the captains on our teams who ended up the degenerate drug addicts, but still, sports and athletics were, before Title IX, maybe still, major vehicles for teaching boys character, right and wrong. I played every sport there was and did all right, mostly won, but I still feel the pain of some of those losses. It hurt like hell. Men don't like to lose to one another. We especially don't like to lose to women.

We just grew up feeling we're supposed to be better than them in sports. The worst thing the coach or one's buddies could call you—worse than "quitter" or "cheater" or "baby"—was "girl." Competing with women pushes very old buttons in us. It's a sort of challenge to prove all over again that there's a difference between boys and girls. We compete extra hard.

The last time I played chess was with a woman. She had me by the rooks until I suckered her into a trap. I think I enjoyed frustrating her hopes for victory "over a man" more than I enjoyed conceiving the moves. I also admired the fervor with which she played, even the panache with which she flung the board against the wall when she realized all hope was lost. She hung in, though, right to the end.

The cardinal rule of competing with a man, if there is one, would be: Do your best, take it seriously, and never quit. The only reason to play a game is to test yourself, see how well you can do. The game is only a metaphor, really, in which you show your pride and your character; and no one wants to play, let alone lose, to someone who has neither.

If you beat me and I seem to be taking it hard, I don't want to be told I had a bad day. If you had fun kicking my butt, saying you enjoyed the match tells me you think I held up my end of the deal, even if you think I'm disappointed in myself. Sports are meant to be talked about afterward, even years later, like the beer commercials on TV where guys get polluted and talk about the high school basketball championship they once watched on TV while drinking beer together. Talk about what happened. Ask him how your service toss looks from his end of the court. Use the device without dwelling on the outcome.

Never apologize. Let his losing be honorable. An apology means you aren't glad to have beaten him, and that's demeaning. The gladder you are to have beaten him (without gloating), the easier it will be for him to believe you respected his effort.

I didn't mind losing to Kari because she had handled herself with grace, acknowledged I'd played well, and didn't act as if beating me was going to hurt our friendship, which I took as a compliment. She was telling me, without actually saying so, that she thought I was bigger than that. As a result, I didn't go off the court saying I'd never play a woman in tennis again. In fact, I'd love to. If I could just find someone with casts on both her legs. And an arm in a sling, maybe. Then I'd have a chance.

When It Goes Wrong

■

Heartbreak I: Lucy

■

Up to that point, she was, without a doubt, the biggest love of my life. Nothing I'd known previously came close to the depths of emotion I felt with Lucy. We met as students in a graduate writing program, and we spent the next three years together. When our relationship fell apart, I fell apart. I would ask myself in wonderment why, if I knew this was going to happen, and I did, was I so surprised, but I was. I felt as though I'd been sitting for years on a train track that I couldn't get off. The fact that you've been sitting on a railroad track for three years doesn't slow down the train that's on it, or make it hurt less when that locomotive finally hits you.

I knew that everything wasn't perfect between us, but I thought all you had to do when the going got tough was get tougher and try harder. I was applying to love the kinds of slogans and aphorisms I'd learned from my high school football coach. I did everything I could to make our relationship work—stupid things like making the apartment Lucy and I shared a nicer place to live in, instead of making myself a nicer person to live with. I did everything I could think of to keep us together, and it exhausted me. Before, I'd succeeded at all kinds of things I barely tried to do or cared about. There were short stories I'd written with ease that made people laugh or cry. I was praised for my drawings, which took no time to do. The one time, though, that I put all my eggs in one basket—and strove with all my might to succeed—I failed. I couldn't believe it.

Had I ignored the warning signs? I think we sense the end is coming, and afterward we're only astonished by how much we chose not to see. The psychology of self-deception is as fascinating as it is complex. One psychologist did a study where the people he was testing were told to watch a film of men passing a basketball and simply count the number of passes made. A woman, wearing a white raincoat, carrying an umbrella, walked right through the middle of the basketball game, but none of the people watching the film could recall seeing her, because they were concentrating on the number of passes. At the same time, a mildly paranoid person afraid of, for instance, fish, could look up at the sky and notice only the clouds thought to resemble fish, most of which, anyone else would say, didn't look like fish at all. In love, because we want love to last, we sometimes find ways not to look directly at the signs that say there's trouble ahead.

We fought. We kept asking each other if we still loved each other, probably asking ourselves, really. I started thinking about other women, that they might save me somehow. I flirted, to test the waters, make myself feel just a little better. We grew indifferent, ending arguments with "I don't care" instead of trying to find solutions. In general, we stopped fighting as much. We spent more time with our separate friends, as if we were setting up support groups, getting them ready. In part I acted like an employee trying to get fired, intentionally doing things she hated, staying out late, refusing to go along with her to a movie or a reading if I didn't feel like it, so that maybe calling it off would be her idea—I was shifting the blame even before there was cause for blame. Maybe she was doing the same thing. Anybody could have seen we didn't smile anymore. Nobody could have seen it, but we didn't make love anymore either.

When Lucy announced that it was over, that it had, in fact, been over for some time, my first reaction was disbelief—then, in a strange way, relief. Okay, I thought, the logjam we'd created had broken. We'd been living in an unsolvable kind of standoff, circumscribed by walls that wouldn't give, no matter how hard we butted our heads against them. Lucy's declaration of dissolution, I concluded, would be a way to shake things up, get the relationship going again. There was a military saying that came out of the Vietnam War, a real Nixonian concept, I always thought, where villages, in order to be saved, had to be destroyed, and it suddenly made sense. Besides, I assured myself, people don't split up for good the very first time they try. Lucy's telling me it was over was like a suicide attempt by a person who doesn't really want to die, but who is actually "crying out for help." I felt sure we'd get back together, and the second time around might be even better than the first. After all, we loved each other. We'd said so right out loud. Love would find a way. She wasn't serious.

A few days later, I found out that Lucy had started a new relationship with another guy, that she was sleeping with him and not at her girlfriend's house, as she'd told me. Suddenly, it dawned on me she was serious about ending our relationship. God, did it dawn on me! Love had found a way all right, but not between Lucy and me.

The night I found out about him, I threw a loony. While Lucy was off somewhere (probably taking refuge in her new boy's arms), I trashed our apartment, kicked a hole in a door, screamed, and threw plants, until the neighbors called the cops, who stopped by to make sure I wasn't hurting anybody but myself. They gave me the number of a counseling hotline. I sat on the floor of the closet and pulled the clothes down around me, screamed until I was hoarse and my throat ached. Finally I called a friend instead. He took me to an all-night truck stop.

My hands shook so badly I could hardly bring the coffee to my lips. The walls were hung with frames of 8 × 10 glossy pictures of trucks. Road-worn grisly drivers glanced at me from time to time with curiosity and disdain. We tried talking it through. The sky was already cobalt blue in the east when he brought me back to the apartment, but I couldn't go in, not because it was a mess. There was a monster in that apartment, and it was out to hurt me. I drove to the house of a married couple I was close to, and they let me sleep in their son's bed. By then, he was getting ready for school, and was puzzled to see me there so early in the morning. I hugged his stuffed animals and cried.

Sometimes it seems women don't believe men are vulnerable. We do act so tough all the time. It's a fraud. I don't care that much when someone I hardly know rejects me, if a woman at a party, for instance, speaks to me for a minute and then looks around for more advantageous fish to fry. It bothers me only for a moment. That person doesn't know me. Lucy knew me better than my parents did, better than anyone ever had. She had all the evidence she needed to make an informed choice. She wasn't just discarding the part of me everyone saw, because she'd seen all of me, naked and weak, good and bad and insecure, all of it. I had nothing to fall back on. All I could say was "No," over and over. My mantra. *"No!"* I wouldn't let it happen. If I could just howl, loud enough, long enough . . .

I couldn't bear being in our apartment again, even for a minute, where everything reminded me of my life with Lucy, so I filled a garbage bag with some clothes and left. For the next month, I slept on the couches and floors of friends. I don't think I ever slept a full eight hours in a row. I lost weight because I had no appetite. I put my life on hold. During the days, I'd help friends out with odd jobs, trying to stay as busy as possible. I played a lot of catch, a lot of pool, and logged hours and hours on video games. I'd go to matinees or stand in a video parlor feeding quarter after quarter into an Asteroids machine, working out aggression by pretending each Asteroid was Lucy. My hands were so shaky that I could actually hit the trigger button better than I ever could before. Eventually, availing myself of a friend for emotional support, and with ten more garbage bags, I packed out of our old apartment and into my art studio, a windowless basement dungeon, complete with stone walls, cobwebs, and spiders, beneath a lawyer's office. There, after business hours, without anybody to hear me, I cried and wailed in the night, screaming at the top of my voice, "I want my home! I want my home!"

I got crazier and crazier. A doctor friend and frequent Asteroids opponent got me a prescription for Valium, but he refused to refill it for me when I'd finished the bottle. I begged him.

Lucy and I divided the town where we lived in half. She got three restaurants and two bars she could go to without worrying that I'd be there, and I got two restaurants and three bars. I was afraid if I saw them together, I'd kill him. I knew I wouldn't really, but I didn't want to admit it, because I'd never hated anybody more. He had what I wanted and hadn't done a thing to get it.

I'd sit in restaurants, realizing I looked exactly like the kind of loser on the skids I used to see and feel sorry for. My hands continued to shake. My penmanship turned into a scrawl, so I'd practice steadying my hands by doodling endlessly on the newspaper pages. I walked and walked, and every shop, café, and street corner in that little town, every place I'd ever been before with Lucy, held tremendous meaning for me. I couldn't believe those same places didn't mean as much to her—that she could go to them with someone else. My friends kept me company when they could, but the distractions never lasted long enough, because sooner or later, I'd have to go home (home?) to my dungeon, alone. I cried every single night and made myself hurt on purpose, intentionally keeping the wounds open, because the pain was all I had the power to hang on to, the only thing I could still control. And I refused to let go of it, because once that was gone, everything was gone.

About three months after the night I lost control, the night I'd first confronted the reality of the separation, if not the finality of it, I decided that finding another woman might make me feel better. At least it would be worth a try. Twice, I took a woman to bed, and both times I ended up crying. It's embarrassing, and it doesn't make the other person feel very good—they're understanding and try to give comfort, but once they're gone you never see them again. You really don't want to do that. You want to keep that sort of thing to a minimum. Finally, one woman, a lot younger than I but with a kind of wisdom from experience that surprised me, told me I didn't need to be with someone—I needed to learn how to be alone. She was right. All the old clichés about learning to like yourself again applied to me now. The question was, How do you start making yourself feel good when you feel so rotten?

The answer came after spending an hour visiting a friend who was laid up in the hospital, a woman who'd had a cyst rupture. I spent an hour not thinking of myself, just trying to make her feel better, and afterward, I realized I was proud of myself for having done it. I determined to do more things I'd be proud of myself for, a kind of forced behavior modification. Maybe this was the resignation stage. I stopped calling up Lucy and picking fights with her. That had made me feel better, but it was getting either of us nowhere, and I was on to a new way to feel better. I stopped driving past our old apartment, looking up to see the lights off, Lucy not at home. I knew I had to break myself of the habit of living near, with, through, or in opposition to her.

If I still felt love for her, I reasoned, it would be better to show it by being a friend, not an adversary. Spend the emotion, instead of letting it build up inside, where the pressure caused pain. I had a mental image of the heart as a steam boiler, and that breaking up had closed one of the valves down. I could still release the pressure by being kind, accepting her definition of the terms. I felt more in charge of my life because now I was helping the division widen—before, it was something happening to me, against my will. I started to get my own work done again too. I let myself cry whenever I felt like it, trying to become an emotional sieve, letting it all pass through me, not clinging to the pain. Eventually, I realized it was time to shut up and stop boring everybody. By then everyone in town, from the butcher to the baker to the candlestick maker, had heard my sad story. Live it through, I said, move on. It was time to load up the car and go, since nothing was keeping me where I was anymore, and there was too much rubble around me to rebuild my life there. It's too hard in a small town—you can't go anywhere without thinking of something you did there, when what you need is *not* to be reminded. I let Lucy have the whole town again. I drove once around the town, smoking a farewell cigar, and then I hit the road, in the tradition of all the devastated men, exiled hearts, who'd ever joined the Foreign Legion, or dragged themselves off into the woods to lick their wounds and face failure alone.

Maybe men fall apart more than women do—a proposition sure to draw fire at a party. As human beings, we experience the same emotions women do (though we may pretend not to), but when it comes to expressing those feelings, we have far fewer emotional role models to follow. The wisdom of football coaches can only take you so far. Maybe heartbreak leaves us more in the dark, more lost. Whoever created male heroes (we create our own, actually) decided that emotion is a weakness, and that pattern holds from Ulysses to Bogey. There's a kind of strength in fictional characters, and then there's the kind you need in real life, a strength that bends and feels and admits weakness, which is real character. The myth says we're allowed to feel anger and lust, some joy, but not grief, especially over a woman. Not for more than a few days. A friend once bragged to me that he'd never cried in his life. Next to bragging that you've never laughed, that's maybe the lamest boast I can think of.

Falling in love, especially for the first time—for real—can set anybody adrift in a sea of emotions strange and wonderful, but once the ship sinks, we learn how truly unseaworthy we are, how helpless and far from shore, with nothing but old lifeboats full of holes to cling to.

The men who seem not to care or feel anything after a breakup have either never felt anything in the first place, or they aren't being completely honest with you. Experience teaches buoyancy, but it's such a hard lesson; a near drowning is a terrifying thing to live through. It took me nearly two years before I found the courage to try the water again. I wanted to be happily alone first, because I remembered that Lucy and I were unhappy people when we met. We'd counted on our relationship for happiness—not ourselves—and that didn't work. The trick is to live well in the present and be as smart as we can be without thinking ourselves to death, trying to guess what will happen next. It was almost a good feeling, once I'd recovered, to know (knock on wood) what the worst thing that could happen feels like, and that I could recover from it.

Heartbreak II: Laurel

■

One of our rituals was lying on the couch, watching "David Letterman," my arms around her, television remote control in one hand, cable remote control in the other. Love in the eighties. One night, they were doing "Stupid Human Tricks," where people balanced eggs on the bridge of their noses or caught coins on their elbows.

"We should go on and do Stupid Couple Tricks," Laurel said one night.

"Like what?" I said. "Moving in together?" We laughed, harder than the joke warranted, because we knew it was so true.

It's not really enough to talk only of what it felt like to get the news, and what the processes were that led to recovery. When you tell someone you broke up, they ask why, and you say, because you don't want to really go into it, "Oh, just little things," little daily problems inherent in living together that add up. A lot of the things Lucy and I went through repeated themselves when I lived with Laurel. You do live and learn, but all the same, even if you've really learned your lesson, you can live and learn the same lesson over and over. People love in patterns, everybody knows: women who only love older men, men who only fall for neurotic women. I love poets from divorced families. Or at least they're who I move in with.

Living together, formerly known as "living in sin" or more formally as "common-law cohabitation" is what people do who believe equally in the possibilities of marriage and the statistical probabilities of divorce, after living apart stops making sense but before sealing the exits and burning all bridges behind you seems prudent. It's a hypothesis.

It's a different kind of marriage. Some people who do it say that, to them, it's the same as being married, but I would guess most people who do it suspect it is not, that marriage is a bigger commitment. Living together is as much of a commitment as the people who do it think they can make, acting on 100 percent of their ability to believe, just like marriage. There's an old-fashioned idea that people who live together are dallying in casual concupiscence, using each other without really caring for each other. It's something that city slickers talk farm girls into doing, an idea usually held by old married couples who resent happy young cohabitants and feel it's not fair that they don't suffer the same hardships married people do. Anybody who knows people who live together knows that they're among the most struggling, self-doubting, insecure, and bewildered people around. They know how hard it is to live with somebody. I think they may take marriage at least as seriously, if not more so, than married people do.

I should say "we," not "they." I am the . . . what's the word? Veteran? Survivor? Benefactor? I have been the male half of two cohabiting experiences, both lasting less than a year. Nobody calls me the Nine-Month Wonder to my face, but I'm starting to think of myself that way.

▪ MONTH ONE ▪

We make the nest.

First we select the nest. It should be in a place where neither of us has lived before, not one person moving in on or encroaching upon another—preferably in a whole new town, a fresh start. Laurel, whom I have known for a year, doesn't want to teach school anymore, and I don't want to live in Rhode Island anymore, so we find a two-bedroom loft on Main Street in a small town in Massachusetts, with a high ceiling in the living room, a view of the mountains, even the extravagance of a sauna built off the bathroom. It's reasonably cheap. I pay more rent because I make more money. It feels strange to me to do that, but I remind myself we are combining our lives. Married people have joint bank accounts. Picture that. I want to do what's fair.

Then we divide up the space, according to need. My idea of a dream house used to be one huge room on a mountaintop with views in all directions, kitchen in one corner, bed in another, work space in the third, living space in the fourth, and a fireplace in the middle. When I mentioned that to the first woman I lived with, she said, "But where's *my* room?" I forgot. I know Laurel will need her own place, somewhere to retreat to and lay claim to, to do anything she wants in, but it's either a corner in the loft or the second bedroom. I need an office to work in, and since I write for a living, while she writes as a student, we agree it's fair that I take the second bedroom. She makes a cozy corner in the loft—a roomy space, but one that can't be closed off.

I set about making the apartment over. I have the time, the tools, and the inclination, while she has to work at her new job, a clerk in a clothing store. I don't mind, since I've been fabricating dreamhouses, in my imagination, since I was little. (My first one looked exactly like the house the Monkees lived in, with barber poles and dentist chairs.) I put up brass towel racks, make coat racks, hat racks, shelves, hang living room shades, install rheostats, wire speakers. Together, we buy lampshades, throw rugs, browse through Crate and Barrel or L. L. Bean catalogues. I buy a vacuum cleaner, the first I've ever bought new, *our* vacuum cleaner, and we get misty-eyed over it. It's all so cute and couple-y.

She complains, though, that my *stuff* (knickknacks, gewgaws, gimcracks, notions, and sundries—all of which I can't live without) overwhelms her *stuff*, that every man she's ever known put his *stuff* everywhere he could and that women throughout history have not been allowed adequate space for their *stuff*, so I leave some of my *stuff* in the closet. Finally, we hang paintings. She doesn't like my favorite oil, which I admit isn't great art and, frankly, I found it in an attic, but at least it's real oil paint, whereas her Picasso poster is great art, but it's still a poster. We hug when we realize it's our first spat. We compromise by hanging them opposite each other. Let them fight it out. She stands back and eyeballs the workmanship, telling me to move it a little to the left, to raise the right corner. When we're done, no crookedly hung paintings anywhere, we light a candle, sip some wine, and realize, in shock, that we are now in *our* home. We get all gooey about it. We kiss, and get carried away on the couch. Finally we blow the candle out and crawl off to sleep in our bed.

Our bed. This is great.

▪ MONTH TWO ▪

We get organized.

It's like learning a complicated dance step, how to move this way when she moves that way, zig when she zags. We reapportion and realign the smaller spaces, sock drawers, kitchen cupboards, silverware trays, and bathroom shelves. We throw our records and tapes together but keep the books separate as well as the closets.

We divide the labor. I used to be democratic about this, and felt that a fifty-fifty split in all chores was fairest, but now I'm a Marxist—from each according to ability, to each according to need. Meaning that as a writer, I have no hours, no boss, no place I usually ever have to be at a given time, so I do the majority of the cleaning, vacuuming, laundry, pickup and fix-up. We make the deal, though, that whoever cooks, the other person does the dishes, which works because Laurel is not big on cooking, while I'm even less big on cleaning up after a meal when I could be watching "Jeopardy" with my feet propped up, digesting my food and soaking up *knowledge*.

We're applying the lessons of coexistence we learned when we were growing up, things our mothers taught us about sanitation, keeping order, being nice. We each have a body of preset notions as to how a loving life is supposed to go, and they serve as a guide.

• MONTH THREE •

We determine how, as a couple, we fit into society at large while operating independently in the general scheme of things.

We become known by the implied ampersand, Peter & Laurel, or Laurel & Peter—like bacon & eggs, thick & thin, Ron & Nancy. We have our friends over to dinner. We don't like each other's friends equally, naturally, but I try not to let it be a bad sign. We become a tighter couple just because now our friends all know us that way. I try not to be on the lookout for bad signs—nothing is perfect, and conflict is to be expected. Like how she leaves her earrings all over the house, bathroom, kitchen, dining room table, in the plants, the dog's bowl. My friend Sandra says men are messy to live with because they have pockets and empty them everywhere. I do this. Forgive and forget, live and let live.

Individually, there are still lives to be lead. In what was tantamount to a panic attack, a month before we moved in together, I called Laurel and tried to warn her about my lifestyle. Everyone lives differently, and getting used to someone else's habits takes time.

I write and can't imagine ever getting a real job, but while it looks easy—a lot of people who see me hanging around think I'm either rich or a bum—it's not. Forget that there are no benefits for free-lancers so you have to pay actual cash from your pocket to your dentist (no novocaine for that pain) or that it's so much a feast or famine proposition that you go flat broke three times a year. It might look as though I'm on a permanent vacation, but in another sense I never am. Some guys go up to their attic to write from nine to five every day and then revel in debasement all night, but I can't do that. If nothing comes to me from nine to five, but then sudden after-dinner inspiration strikes, I have to work then. When the Muse calls, you have to answer the phone, or you go broke for good and have to live in a dumpster, talking to your wine. If I get huge amounts of work done during the day, then sometimes

I can let up and focus on other people at night, but otherwise, I'm pretty much distracted and antsy, my natural state.

The structures I superimpose help organize what would otherwise be a completely fluid life. Typically, I don't lie around in bed, not even on Saturdays or Sundays. The lower my bank account goes, the earlier I rise. I shower (forcing myself, now that I live with someone, to remember not to use all the hot water). I dress, and then I go to a restaurant, the same one every day, for breakfast, where I order my usual and then read the paper. Reading the paper and drinking oceans of coffee gets my brain started. Once my brain is started, then and only then can I take out a legal pad and start writing for a few hours. I go home to *process* what I wrote in the morning, wait for the mailman, clean and putz, or I simply stand in the middle of the apartment staring mindlessly at a fixed point in space. It's important, though, to start each day the same way.

One morning, toward the end of our third month, I ask her if she wants to come to breakfast with me, before she goes off to her real job.

"Why?" she says.

"What do you mean, why?" I say. "For the pleasure of your company."

"You don't want my company," she says. "You just want to read the paper and be by yourself. There's nothing pleasurable about eating breakfast with you. I'd rather eat alone than sit and be ignored."

"But . . ." I begin.

The honeymoon is over.

• MONTH FOUR •

The second trimester is one of testing, push coming to shove.

It begins with the mutual realization that this relationship is not going to be a bowl of cherries. We both knew better than to think, going in, that love comes without effort. I had dearly hoped that this relationship would require as little as possible. I dreamed of the perfect fit. So did she. Judgment can no longer be suspended, once we both know that one of us is unhappy about something.

"I always wanted to be one of those couples you see lounging around in cafés, reading the paper or writing and looking contented," I say.

"Sitting in a restaurant ignoring each other is not my idea of fun," she says. She always wanted to be one of those couples that find everything they need in each other, that talk intimately with infinite animation all the time.

"I can't do that," I say. "Going to breakfast for me is just like any other working person going to the office. I have to separate myself."

"Fine," she says. "Just don't invite me, because I don't want to be taken for granted."

"I *want* to take you for granted!" I shout. "I want you to take me for granted. What *alternative* are you proposing? You think we should be *nervous* and self-conscious and *insecure* and constantly *worried* about the relationship and where it's going all the time? Is that the *desired goal* here?"

▪ MONTH FIVE ▪

I'm nervous and self-conscious and insecure and constantly worried about the relationship and where it's going all the time. She is too.

I really tried not to be this way. I'm happiest when I'm not *trying* to think of what I'm doing wrong or what I should do to please her, but I know I have to. "Oh, you *have to?*" Laurel says. "It's an afterthought to concern yourself with me? That's what I'm getting at," she says. "There's just not the kind of *empathy* I expected."

"You can expect sympathy," I say. "You can't expect empathy, because I don't have ESP. I love you and I care about you, and I try to be considerate, but I can't guess what you're feeling. Maybe I'm self-centered, but I want you to be happy."

We agree to work on the way we communicate.

Part of the problem here is that I'm older than she is. She's worried about where she's going in life, what her true vocation is, how to get there. I'm not worried, because everyone I know went through that, and sooner or later, almost everyone I know got over that. I promise her it levels off when you hit thirty. She worries about money. I say don't worry about money. I've got some and I know where to get more. People with less than we have get by fine. She feels I'm cold, when she has a problem or a crisis and I don't respond the way she wants, but I learned, the first time I lived with anyone, that you have to say, once in a while, "That's your problem—you deal with it," rather than serve as each other's excuses. Besides, I don't want to be the one who solves anything for her. I want her to find her own way. She wants that too, of course. I'm not trying to be cold. I'm trying to apply what I think I know.

We go three or four days of having calm fun together, punctuated by vigorous efforts to communicate. She still works all day and generally wants to stay home at night. I'm still home all day and want to go out at night. We go out together, more than she ever used to, to movies or to concerts, and we stay home together, more than I ever used to, but even so, the difference in schedules and energy levels takes its toll. We wake together, but I frequently stay up two or three hours after she goes to bed. Sometimes we both watch Letterman, but when she crashes at eleven, leaving me to my own devices, faced with the choice of watching Johnny Carson or Ted Koppel, reading (but that's lonely too), or walking the dog around the corner to the local pub and having a beer with friends, I'd sooner go out. We communicate about this.

"Why shouldn't I be insecure," she says, "when you have to go out every night?"

"Not *every* night," I say. "I don't *have* to. I enjoy it, it's true, but what's it to you anyway? You're asleep."

"I work."

"So do I," I say. "The point is, I'm with you for as long as you're conscious." And if she were awake, but I just wanted to go out and be alone, wouldn't that be all right too, every now and then? I like her company, but I like sitting alone in public as well.

"I can't stay up or go out every night," she says.

"I can't go to bed before I'm tired," I say. "I hated it when I was a kid and I had to go to bed during daylight saving time and it was still light out, and I hate it now. It's like being in prison."

"Well, grow up then."

"Exactly," I say. "Adults get to go to bed when they want to."

"I hate you." I'm not empathizing. She feels all alone.

"Why?" I say. "I'm not doing anything wrong—I'm an honorable person. You think I'm off having affairs or something? I never do anything I wouldn't do if you were there. I want you there. If you want to sleep, that's fine, but just don't tell me to sit still in a chair while you sleep, because that time is mine."

"I just don't want to be anxious," she says.

"Then don't feel anxious," I say. Oh sure, as if you can just snap your fingers and make it go away. Maybe with time. "Have faith in yourself, or trust me, or whatever you have to do."

It's Johnny Carson's lousy writers. It's everything, my boredom, a restlessness I've felt my whole life, from the hyper toddler to the crazed teenager to the insomniac college student and on and on. It's a craving to talk to people, possibly meet new ones, after being alone all day, just absorb something external and get away from being creative for a living. "It's just me," I say. "I'm sorry. I can't help it." She says she understands. We kiss and make up, but deep down, she's asking herself if she wants to live with this, if this represents an acceptable level of work on her part. Probably not.

▪ MONTH SIX ▪

Nobody makes the bed anymore.

She has mood swings, pretending for as long as she can that things are going to be okay, then angry and frustrated because the problems don't go away. She warned me, in a panic-attack phone call similar to the one I made before we moved in, that she could be moody. I can't tell what's going to happen next, and I no longer trust that her being cheerful means anything—swinging back and forth from optimism to pessimism is killing me.

Between the different clocks we live by, and the arguing, and the desire we both have to pull free of each other just for a day or a night, to catch our breath and find temporary peace of mind, we start orbiting each other. Six months, and we already need separate vacations. Our sex life suffers. We still love each other, but it's hard to feel unconflictingly in love with each other at the same time. We don't know what's happening.

"We're out of phase," I say.

"It's all right," she says, knowing it isn't.

I drive around a lot. I feel ridiculously tense at home, and so does she. Driving around, I realize I don't want to go home, not if I'm going to feel that anxious. I love her, but it's hard to be with her. We're both asking ourselves if we want to live this way. Definitely not. But is there a way out? If it's not right, it's not right. I retreat from that position. It's not *always* tense at home. We're just out of phase.

I have to go to Montana on assignment, to write an article about fly fishing for a doctors' magazine. She gets incredibly nervous before I leave. She tells me she never bargained for living with someone who was going to go away for weeks at a time. I can't believe this—I never hid what I did for a living. Of course I'd have to go away from time to time. She says if I ever had to spend a whole summer away, doing an article or a book, she wouldn't trust the relationship enough to stay with it. I say if I got a great offer to do a book traveling somewhere for a summer, I'd have to do it, and wouldn't want a relationship so weak and insecure that I'd have to worry about it at the expense of my career.

We apologize long distance over the phone. While I'm gone, she relaxes and gets piles of her own work done, becomes productive, enjoys herself, feels fulfilled and empowered, out from under. I tell her she's supposed to feel that way all the time. We don't understand why she can't, with me around. She feels as though she's giving up. While I'm gone, she sees no harm in perusing the apartments-for-rent section of the want ads. This is the turning point. She knows she doesn't want to live with me.

• MONTH SEVEN •

The last trimester is extrication and withdrawal, denial and acceptance, alleviated by short respites of cosmic sadness where you hold each other close and stare out different windows, wondering why exactly the opposite of what you both wanted to happen is happening.

Conversations begin, "I must have said this a million times, but you still don't understand that . . .", and end, ". . . we're just different people." The level of intimacy that satisfies me clearly doesn't satisfy her. Spending a few hours doing anything together— eating, walking around, reading books on opposite ends of the couch, or watching television—is enough to leave me feeling well-fed, but it leaves her hungry. We argue about who is more romantic, the one who finds satisfaction in less or the one who dreams of more. She wants more than a few hours, comes home from work craving closeness, but, time and again, doesn't get it, or enough of it when we are together. There's a person five feet from me. She wants something from me. What? Why can't I know?

One night she's sullen and withdrawn. I ask her what's wrong. She tells me what she needs, in ultimatum-like tones, as if she feels there's nothing left to lose. I say she can't demand that I meet 100 percent of her needs, that it's usually an illusion that anyone can, really. I never promised a rose garden, or something like that. *Life* doesn't promise that. You don't have to settle for less, exactly, but with experience you learn to place greater value on the 85 percent that is right about someone else, and not get all bent out of joint about the 15 percent that isn't. As a friend of mine said, "Eighty-five? Geez, I'd settle for fifty."

She tells me I don't even think the relationship is important enough to even want to change for it. She says we should see a counselor. "I've seen counselors before," I say. "There's nothing magical about them." My hunch is, they'd only lead us to admitting what we already know. "What makes me hard to live with is what makes me productive—it's what makes me me. Same thing with you. No, I don't want to change—I'm all right, just like this. Take me or leave me. You get older, you start thinking that way. I'm faithful, I care, I'm on your side all the way, I believe in you— what more do you want? I never asked you to change. If you want to change, all you get is the way people change to suit each other over a *long* period of time, not drastic personality alternations in seven months." She tells me I'm ridiculously well-defended. I say why shouldn't I be? She adopts a sarcastic tone and says that must be why I'm so happy all the time. I say I am happy, except when I'm worried about someone else being unhappy because of me. Her happiness is her job, not mine, I shout. I tell her to do what she needs to be happy, write a novel, change careers, go to grad school— take care of herself. It's not my fault. I can't stand it.

"I just want to live with a happy person," I say.

"Maybe you should just live alone then," she says.

"Maybe I should."

"Maybe we both should," she says. "I think I want to move out."

Take me or leave me? Did *I* say that? Allow me to retreat from that position. . . .

▪ MONTH EIGHT ▪

It's just part of the getting of wisdom, whether you want it or not, learning to cut your losses, fold the cards, and go home, but what you have to forfeit, beyond your innocence, is your idealism. Not all of it but some. The first time someone told me "I think I want to move out," I fought it with all my might, told myself, "Well, she only says she *thinks* she wants to move out." I begged her to stay, saw counselors, did whatever I could think of. But now it's the second time. I know Laurel doesn't just *think* she wants to move out. She wants to. I tell myself if she feels that strongly about it, then she probably should. It seems odd to take her so readily at her word, as if I'm a quitter now, a victim of creeping cynicism. My spirit flags quickly these days. I don't want to cause pain or feel it.

We continue to fight, of course, just to maintain our positions, for posterity, or pride, but without hope of altering an inevitable course of events. I get told one day that I don't talk about my feelings, so I throw a drawerful of magazine articles I've written about my feelings at her and say, "Compared to who—Joe the Plumber?" We talk about the ways we talk, that I dominate and criticize in speech while she defers and supports, so I shout at her that that's absurd because I've never had the slightest doubt she wasn't the brightest, funniest woman I've ever met, and I love hearing her talk, and if she wants to dominate and criticize back, "then go right ahead, be my guest!" Something in the way I shout this seems dominating and critical to her. God, I say, I'm just trying to talk.

"What do you want a relationship for?" she asks, finally. The question stings. "I mean, really, it's like you'll take one at *your* convenience, for a few hours a day, on *your* terms, and the rest of the time, you do what *you* want."

"I don't know," I say. It's true. My terms are not the same as her terms. We both want it our own way. We're each getting about half what we desire, which on paper would look equitable (if not blissful), but this is not on paper.

She starts picking up her earrings and putting away her clothes more often, not to appease me but for her own sake. Now that we know the jig is up, we both pull back into ourselves. She gets writing done, sings with a jazz trio, visits friends in New York, and accomplishes a lot more than she did when she allowed herself to be preoccupied with the problem of Us. To her way of thinking, she's happier because she's giving up. She thinks of herself first now, not me, and doesn't, therefore, feel it's love according to how she's always defined it. To her, love means sacrifice, selflessness, constant involvement with the other person, constant giving. I don't really argue, since I was raised with similar values, but it's also sort of a pre-feminist situation where she makes herself second to me, and she is a politically astute person. It's confusing. She can't put herself first and love me at the same time. Some days I feel as if to her I'm hardly me at all, not a man singular but all men, who (as when I say a woman I see on the street has gorgeous hair) reduce women to sex objects and make them feel insecure about their looks (though on a personal level she enjoys compliments and praise as much as anyone, as much as I do). The times when she says, "It's not you, it's me—I just need to find some things out about myself," I know she means it, even though it's what everybody says when they break up, and I just wish she could do whatever it is she has to do without feeling I'm preventing her. I wanted to be there.

"Maybe we should try again," she says one night in bed. "What do you think?"

"Oh God," I say. We're each pulled in two directions. "How can I get my hopes up again? A year from now, the same incompatibilities would be there, wouldn't they? I couldn't go on, thinking that any day you'd want to break it off again."

"I know," she said. "We can't keep doing this to each other."

She looks at me. She was so sure I was right for her. I was so sure she was right for me. Now I'm sure I'm not, that someone else would truly be better for her, someone with the same need for intimacy. She can't stop believing in him anyway, wherever he is.

"I'll be out by the end of next month."

▪ MONTH NINE ▪

We try to be cheerful and ensure that life goes on, in spite of this looming major change. The irony is bizarre, but this month is one of our happiest. We don't get on each other's cases anymore. At last we know what's going to happen. It's hard to tell where acceptance leaves off and denial picks up, but we talk now.

"Maybe you should go a year without a relationship, just as an experiment," I say.

"You shouldn't think of yourself as a freak that no one could ever live with," she tells me. "I'm just neurotic."

"Not compared to a lot of people I know," I say.

"I bet we'd work out if we'd met three years from now," she says.

I wonder if we still would. Where will I be in three years?

When I play a record or a tape, I start putting them back into her pile or my pile when I'm done. I eyeball how many boxes we have lying around, how many she'll need. I wonder if I'll have to move or if I can afford the apartment alone. I go my first month ever where my American Express card bill is $0.00, and to celebrate, I mail them a check made out for *nothing*. They offer me a Gold Card immediately. I make no expensive long-distance phone calls. I buy no clothes or toys. I think about trips I can take, or all the work I'll be able to get done. I think how much I'll miss her, how you really don't know what you've got until it's gone. We both know we're going to be sorry, but we have to play the thing out.

"Tell me when you're going to pack out," I say. "I'd like to not be here to watch it happen."

"Okay," she says. We're snuggled in bed. I keep trying not to think that this is the nth to the last time we'll sleep together here in our home. I half pretend she won't leave, but she will. She should. I feel like I'm going out of my mind.

"It'll be okay," I say.

"I know," she says. "It'll be fine."

"I just really can't imagine doing anything different, if we could do it all over."

"I can't either," she says.

▪ EPILOGUE ▪

I wonder all the time what difference being married would make.
The notion that you should get married so it will be harder to break
up still sounds about as logical as making more and more, larger
and larger hydrogen bombs so you won't ever use them. Would I
take things even more for granted? Would she trust me more and
feel more secure? Would I feel even more restless and trapped?
Would the new definition of myself as "Married Man" (sounds like
a superhero) give me a more secure anchor? A married buddy told
me, "When you're married, you're able to weather much larger
crises, but then you're more likely to have them in the first place."

I would consider living with someone again just because nothing
else I could do would adequately inform someone of what it's like
to live with me, before making the larger leap. You can talk yourself
blue in the face, trying to warn each other, and you can swear you
can live with anything, but you can't know until you try. I don't
consider living with Laurel a failure. Every failed experiment is a
positive finding in another sense, I know, or as Churchill said,
"Success is going from failure to failure with no loss of enthusiasm."

You memorize little slogans like that and repeat them to make
yourself feel better, but then one day you drop your sunglasses
behind the couch cushion, and when you reach in to get them,
you find an earring, and then you lose it all over again. Regret-
lessness is just a pose. Then I wish we'd gotten married, because
while it lasted, it was often sad but otherwise so good and rich and
interesting, so strong a love, if not the right kind of love, that
telling people later that "we lived together but she moved out"
makes it seem way too small, casual, and insignificant, when in
fact we took the biggest chance we could, and made the biggest
love we were capable of making.

Departing Flights:
How to Dump Me

∎

The first time I ever got dumped was in high school, by a girl I'll call Mary Hanson. All she said was "I'm dropping you." It could have been worse. When a friend of mine in high school, Gary, was going to drop his girlfriend Beth, he told her at a party, "Hey, Beth, guess what? I'm *dropping you* at midnight!" Then he gave her a countdown for the entire party, "Hey, Beth, you got two more hours. . . . Hey, Beth, ten minutes!" Even so, I thought Mary had been plenty cold to me. I couldn't believe life could be so cruel, and I bawled my eyes out in my bedroom. Then, in that trembling, vulnerable state, I went downstairs, turned on the TV, and watched "Hee Haw" for the first and only time in my life. It made me feel much better. Tell you the truth, I laughed my butt off.

When you grow up, you learn that "Hee Haw" is not always going to do the trick. Perhaps "parting is such sweet sorrow" for lovers who know they'll meet again as lovers, but when you're certain that's not going to happen, parting isn't sweet in the least.

I suggest again that men are no better equipped emotionally to handle rejection than women are. The guys who strike stoic poses and re-armor themselves aren't recovered—they're incompletely healed at best. My old roommate, upon getting dumped, worked six ten-hour shifts a week for two years and smoked dope until he was tired enough to sleep almost every night to forget the whole thing. It's a painful process that gets set in motion, and it will go on causing pain for a while, but how long that pain lasts will depend on just how a woman lets a man down.

There's no great way to break the news except to make sure she tells him herself and doesn't let him find out the hard way, come home and find apartments for rent circled in the want ads open on the coffee table, or even hear it from a third party. Too fast and hard is as bad as too slow and soft. Think of it as like having a tooth removed—you don't really want it to sit there hurting until it falls out on its own, but you don't want it yanked out either. It's wrong to declare to him that the relationship is over, with only a vague explanation of why, and then unplug the phone, thinking that's a nicer approach than dragging it out. You don't want to be indecisive or inconsistent either, blowing hot and cold, believing the relationship will work one day and laboring to convince yourself it's fine, and maybe convince him, then saying no, I was right in the first place, it isn't working.

Suppose I fall in love with someone, but it doesn't work. Just suppose. Once she's concluded that the relationship has to end, I would like (and I think most men would like) it to happen this way. First, I'd like to know that it's coming. I would simply prefer some advance notice. "Let's get together Monday night, because we need to talk [insert dramatic pause] about us." Delivered in the right tone, this can only mean one thing and if I'm against it, I'll have time to anticipate what she'll say and prepare a response. If I'm in agreement, I'll have time to catalogue the good memories and review them, put them in order and pack them away. Either way, I'll know not to buy theater tickets for Tuesday night.

Next, I want the reasons explained to me, voiced in as much science as possible. Men are good at converting the emotional to the rational, which may not always serve us well, but it's still the best way for us to understand. In the end, all that really matters is that you don't feel good in a relationship, but men want to see linear cause and effect.

I don't want a list of my bad habits; this isn't the time to tell me what's wrong with me, but rather what's right *with* me but wrong *for* you. I want to believe we're victims, like Rick and Ilsa in *Casablanca*, of destiny, not of puny differences. "It couldn't ever work because I like to go places while you'd rather spend your time quietly at home." "You need a talker and I'm a listener." "It's not us, it's *it*." Men will buy this. Letting me think something about the relationship wasn't working—not something about me—leaves me room to retreat with my pride intact.

I want a last kiss. Even if all the love is gone, I want to know she remembers that love was there, and I don't want to go away wondering when we kissed last. People have used rituals since snakes walked to mark the beginnings of things, like births or weddings, and the endings of things, like funerals. A ritual performed for passages and transitions marks their place in history, sets them apart from the endless blend of events in time so that they won't be lost in memory. I tend to run through my memories all the time, to gauge where I am now, or who. I want a last kiss.

Then I want the option of a weaning schedule. To me, a gradual separation is better than cold turkey. I want to know exactly when she'll come to my apartment to get her things. I want to know that I can phone her if I need to talk. I do not, initially, really want to hear about new guys, but I do want to follow as an observer, for a while, the life I used to participate in. Maybe it will make it seem more like redefining and reorganizing the relationship than ending it, though that could be just hanging on, which isn't healthy.

When I'm doing the dumping, I try to apply the same rules, and be clear and consistent, not blame, and show class wherever possible. I think of how I'm going to be remembered. If I'm angry or bitter at someone, I try hard to be as forgiving as possible and not show it. Let her go on with her life with as good an outlook as she can.

Ultimately, a woman probably has to hurt a man to leave him, but she doesn't have to show him less kindness on the way out than she did on the way in. *Casablanca* is a testament to class romance, start to finish. Tell me we'll always have Paris, and get on the plane. Let me remember how good it was, not the hurt.

Happy Trails

∎

"**C**an we meet somewhere?" Barbara says. "I have to talk to you about something—you're the only person who will understand."

"Oh I am, am I?" I *want* to say. "So now that you've gone two months without me, you suddenly start to appreciate the two years you spent with me, right? And you think you can call me up any time you want and I'll come running just like things were still the same, you heartless manipulating cold neurotic petty treasonous witch-cow-whore. . . ."

"Sure," I say, "I'd love to."

I mean this sincerely.

In high school, the phrase "Can we just be friends?" meant, "Buzz off, Jim's got a 'vette and you don't," and my response was usually something like, "Sure, we can be friends, as long as I don't ever have to see you again." Even now, reverting to "just friends" can seem like an exercise in masochism, a way of painfully reminding yourself of the beating you took on your emotional investment. When you break up with someone, either you feel guilty or you blame the other person. Guilt and blame are lousy drinking buddies.

At the same time, no one knows you better than an ex-lover, because you trusted each other more than you trusted anyone. Often, no one is capable of being more sympathetic than an ex-

157

lover. Sometimes, no one can give you better advice, remind you of your flaws, or tell you what your strengths are. Unless you were completely wrong about your ex's character, there had to have been *something* good you saw there, which, if it was strong enough to base a whole love affair on, could be strong enough to base a friendship on.

So I drive to meet Barbara. I ask myself, Why am I doing it? Because I want to think of myself as a reliable friend in need. I also want to show her, by being nice, that she was wrong to leave me—so she'll feel worse. Hopefully. Every good, selfless reason has a bad, selfish other reason attached to it. Maybe I just want to unmix the emotions.

"Hi, Pete-Pete," she says, taking my hand. It stirs me, just a little, to hear her call me what she used to call me.

"What's this mysterious thing that only I can understand, that none of the jerks you've been dating since me can't?" I say. I rehearsed this line all the way in the car.

"It's Andrea," she says, rolling her eyes.

I'm a little disappointed it's not boy trouble. I was there for the beginning of Barbara's problems with her neurotic friend Andrea, so I listen to the latest chapter. She always sought my advice on this sort of thing, and I'm glad she still needs me for it. She seems at ease with me, more as I remember her from the early, golden days. I hate to admit it, but she looks better, healthier, happier too.

"Been to the beach lately?" I say. "You look tan."

"Yeah," she says.

"With whom?"

"Remember Alan? That blond guy you said was a creep? I went with him." I feel a sick, sinking feeling in my gut. I guess I really didn't want to hear about her new situation. "I don't know if I really want to see him again, though. All he ever does is talk about himself."

"Give him a chance," I say. "He's probably just trying to impress you."

I can hardly believe I'm saying this. Giving her advice on how to get something going with someone else. Yet we both decided to move on, and a friend would help her do that. It's forced and bizarre, but it's going to have to be, isn't it? For a while, at least.

Driving home, I almost feel that endeavoring to make the friendship work will be as important as it once was to make the relationship work. There's a kind of friendshp that only ex-lovers can have, one that surpasses simple friendship, sort of the ultimate Plan B. Barbara knows what side of the bed I sleep on, where I keep my forks, all the little things. Which wire to jiggle on the battery when my car won't start. I know the details of her life too. I can be friends with her on more levels than I can be friends with practically anyone else I know.

Some people, of course, you just can't see, if it's too harsh, too fresh, or too sad. But if you can continue in the commitment you made to each other's happiness, not because you want to get anything out of it for yourself but just for the pleasure of making someone else happy, then you can convert a loss into a gain. You can skip over the incompatibilities you could not avoid when you were working toward the future side by side, and come at it separately, with each other's help.

I stay friends in another way. I have always doted on the memories I have of past relationships. It's always seemed so natural to talk about them, use anecdotes from them to illustrate a point I might want to make regarding a current relationship, sometimes to the concern and/or dismay of current relations. Past relationships, in a way, are as important as the current ones, because they are where I learned everything I know. For me, the bitterness fades quickly, and a lasting sentimental attachment sets in. Old lovers are like old war buddies, the people I teamed up with for as long as it lasted, to face the world and see what we could do with it. I dream sometimes of us all getting together, having a reunion, sort of a living version of the Frenchman's fantasy to have a funeral crowded with his weeping mistresses. Maybe have a big house in the country where we can all live together. All of *their* past lovers, needless to say, are not welcome, because in my fantasy they only want to be with me. Which is why in reality (and in realty) I'm not in the market for a big house in the country. It's only in my imagination, a big solid house where we all peacefully coexist, trade off household chores, and continue, side by side by side by side.

Postscript

■

Ordinary Joe

■

The title of this book makes sport of the notion that there's an image, a standard of reality, which modern men should live up to, and by doing so stands to suggest that we remain confused or in disagreement as to what it's supposed to be. I know I am, though it's not trendy to admit to confusion anymore. They say there's a new guy on the block, that Macho is back. The New Male of the eighties, Mr. Macho, has supplanted the Sensitive Man of the seventies, as characters like Ollie North, Rambo, or Ronald Reagan become known and lionized for their sheer single-mindedness (simplemindedness), their ability to extricate themselves from the malaise of Jimmy Carter, where Sensitive Man felt so at home. Heroes throughout history have been decisive. Hamlet is just as dead at the end of the play as everybody else, but at least he finally made his mind up.

The New Macho is ka-ka. Maybe the image reflects a national mood swing, and maybe everybody is dressing a little snappier now, and maybe we're all just a little more dissatisfied with our ordinary lives when we compare them to glittery beer commercials in slow motion, but past that, the idea is deep as a cookie sheet, no better than a facade behind which new men hide from new women. It's still a malaise, because women really have changed in the last twenty-five years, a fact the New Real Macho Man runs in terror from, and Ordinary Joes think about a good part of the time. Fortunately, most of the actual male human beings I know think the

163

New Macho is nonsense too and know we can't, nor should we want to, ignore what's happened in the last quarter century. Judging from the men I know, we think feminism is here to stay, we think it's good that it is, and we're just not sure all the time where that leaves us. We've been conditioned in innumerable ineffable ways, and we fight change just like anybody resists the unfamiliar. But as far as I can testify, real men, actual male human beings, are still trying to be sensitive, are still confused, still trying to synthesize past and present, and are no more macho than we ever were.

So who is Ordinary Joe?

Ordinary Joe wonders what happened. There are plenty of guys out there who still find sexual equality a threat, who blame feminism for changing the status quo and want to keep their women at home making babies or dinner. A friend having marital troubles once told me, "I don't get it—all I need to be happy is food on the table when I come home from work and a little sex now and then— I'm so easy to please—why isn't she?" Because she's evolved and he hasn't. Women expect more, these days. Ordinary Joe hopes she doesn't expect it from him.

Ordinary Joe wants a woman who is already happy, who is doing something that fulfills her. He wants a woman with a job or career, so there will be more money. There are relationships, consequently, that suffer sexually because now there are two people who can say, "Not tonight, I had a bad day at the office," instead of one. Stress is anathematic to sex, whatever the gender. He wants a woman with a job, but without stress. He wants a woman who enjoys sex and feels in charge of her own sexuality. The fantasy of submitting passively to a sexually aggressive woman is quite common among men. There's a sense of being relieved of the responsibility of making the act occur, and a dramatic amplification of everything about sex that men find pleasurable and positive, the feeling of being overwhelmed and consumed by the power of it, without fear of failure.

It's also true that a sexually aggressive woman can increase the pressure a man feels to perform, the imperative to become enabled.

The more a woman wants from Ordinary Joe, the more self-conscious he'll be, so he will give off mixed signals. He wants to have his cake and eat it too. In the old days, men wanted complete control over the sexual experience, and tried to orchestrate the encounter in the only way they knew it would work for them by setting up familiar conditions, resisting deviation from the norm, which leads to self-consciousness, which leads to failure. This is a kind of psychological construction men probably won't ever be able to escape entirely. On balance I think Ordinary Joe wouldn't mind a woman initiating sex, particularly since he knows that the old notion, "she says no but she means yes" doesn't hold water anymore, and consent is required by common decency. Personally, it's knowing I'm exciting someone else that excites me, the feedback loop of mutually increasing expectations that I focus in on, not who had the idea first. If she did, that's good; it means she likes me. But if I do, and she doesn't get caught up in the spirit, forget it, I'd rather watch "David Letterman." Or if she does, but I don't feel the time is right, I want that to be okay too.

Ordinary Joe still doesn't want to go to men's encounter groups. He wants to be honest with his pals, but he doesn't want to be touchy-feely with other men. Men just don't say anything meaningful to each other unless they're really drunk. Sometimes while jogging together. It's tradition. None of my friends has ever said he felt satisfied with the amount of sexual information given to him by his father. Mothers have to tell girls something, because the consequences of not telling them anything are too dire, or because women don't compete the way men do. Boys, who often can't imagine asking their fathers anything in the first place, since they learn not to ask before they learn exactly *what* not to ask, look mainly to other boys, to see how they're supposed to behave, sexually, and it's worse than the blind leading the blind, because the blind are usually willing to admit they're blind. Boys lie. Spend five minutes in a fraternity house, if you dare, and you can see how late into life boys still need to be around each other, practicing to be men, sanctioning each other, testing (without admitting it) to see if what they think they think they know is correct, and okay, because they still don't know exactly what to do. They say men hit their sexual peak at twenty, but it's hard to imagine whoever says that is talking about anything other than sperm counts or cardiovascular capacity. Men my age (in their thirties) are much better at talking about sex with each other, but we still address the subject in a kind of detached, clinical way, sprinkled with humorous anecdotes to diffuse the tension. Sometimes feelings and doubts come out, but usually no deep true confessions, not the way we're all sure women talk all the time. And it still helps to have had a few beers. For what it's worth, a woman I know who grew up in Germany says Italian men really are the best lovers, because they don't mind talking with each other about how to please women.

Ordinary Joe wants to be told he's the greatest lover in the world, even when he's not Italian. He wants his lover to have all the orgasms she wants, because it's thrilling to be able to give them. Then again, where hers are multiple and his is single, the odds are, he'll be more likely to say enough is enough first than she will. There are only so many hours in a day. What makes a good lover, for me, is a woman who is equal parts generous and selfish, eager to please and be pleased, and the more so the better. There was a woman I knew, a poet, who was quite consciously endeavoring to write about a vigorous, bold sort of female sexuality, "legs wrapping around doorways," and to live the poems out, while remaining a committed feminist. I wrote a poem back to her that had the line, "when we kiss, we exchange teeth," and it was almost true. She was always more in control than I felt I was, leading me to bed by the tie once, as I recall, and she was totally unpredictable, which I both liked and felt driven crazy by. Measuring lovers against performance standards is really stupid, though, and I think Ordinary Joe knows that. It's like singing—not everyone can be Pavarotti, or even sing on key all the time. Or it's like comparing mountains, or sunsets—all different, all spectacular.

Ordinary Joe is not sexually sure of himself, as the New Macho would have it, because O.J. still has his unpredictable appendage to deal with. D. H. Lawrence called him John Thomas, making the penis seem to have a will and a mind of its own. Some women think this is a scam.

It's true. In fact, just the other day, I caught mine ordering camping equipment from a mail-order catalogue and charging it on its own VISA card. *I* can't even get VISA. A survey of my friends found that nine out of ten men when asked, "How integrated do you feel with your John Thomas?" will make jokes, and the other one will feel too ashamed or self-conscious to laugh.

Ordinary Joe believes there are things we can't ever really know about each other. Men can't know what it's like to be pregnant, and women can't know what it's like to have an organ which is half voluntary, half involuntary. We're in a much better position to understand penises than you are, and *we* don't even know what's going on, sometimes.

It does often feel as if the penis acts of its own accord, and raises questions about our bodies that we may not want to answer, not right when the question is being asked, during sex, since sex is one of the least rational or intellectual things we do, just behind pro wrestling. The integration isn't between a man and his penis—it's between a man's thoughts and emotions. The word "integration," though, is as good a metaphor as any for what it's like when everything goes right, the consciousness listening to the unconscious, feelings in harmonious balance with thought.

Ordinary Joe is glad that women have arrived (or are still arriving) at a new understanding of themselves, a new empowerment, both social and sexual. He knows this is good for her, but what is it for him? If there is a way to put the New Macho in a positive light, it would be to suggest that it's nothing more than men wanting to enjoy their sexuality the same way women can, that it doesn't really ignore the women's movement as much as it exists in response to it. Women have gained power, so Ordinary Joe wants to gain power too. This is why Ordinary Joe is confused, because he wants to do the right thing but he wants to enjoy himself as well, to feel good about his life. My friends, just regular middle-class college-educated working palookas, all seem to be looking for the compromise and keep asking themselves, What does feminism mean to me, to this particular relationship, wives or girlfriends, on this given day?

The New Man of the eighties appears to have stopped asking the question. Maybe there are real guys like that, but I don't know them. The New Man's a cartoon, one-dimensional. Most people have more depth than that.